AD PRIMERS

Context

AD PRIMERS

Context

Architecture and the Genius of Place

ERIC PARRY

WILEY

To A. A. P. and I. M. P.

Registered office
John Wiley & Sons Ltd, The Atrium, Southern Gate, Chichester, West Sussex, PO19 8SQ, United Kingdom

For details of our global editorial offices, for customer services and for information about how to apply for permission to reuse the copyright material in this book please see our website at www.wiley.com.

ISBN 978-1-119-95271-8 (paperback)
ISBN 978-1-118-94673-2 (ebk)
ISBN 978-1-118-94674-9 (ebk)
ISBN 978-1-118-94567-4 (ebk)

Executive Commissioning Editor: Helen Castle
Project Editor: David Sassian
Assistant Editor: Calver Lezama

Cover design, page design and layouts by Karen Willcox, www.karenwillcox.com
Printed in Italy by Printer Trento Srl

Cover photograph by Dirk Lindner

MIX
Paper from responsible sources
FSC® C015829
www.fsc.org

Acknowledgements

A book of this kind, like designing a building or directing a film, is made up of a complex web of parts, and here the actors are those who have participated; my most significant debt is for the time they allowed me in discussing their projects, particularly Álvaro Siza, Adam Caruso and Peter St John, Shelley McNamara and Yvonne Farrell, Lisa Fior, and Peter and Anneliese Latz. The stimulus to write has been a desire to add a bridge between practice, which consumes my daily life, and the academic discourse of architectural and urban studies. In the latter I am lucky to have long-standing friendships with outstanding contributors: Dalibor Vesely who encouraged me from the outset, Peter Carl, Bob Maxwell, Wilfried Wang and David Leatherbarrow with their boundless generosity, Joseph Rykwert and Richard Sennett through their writings and conversation.

The chapter on the kinetics of the street is the beginning of a broader study that was stimulated by the Theatrum Mundi group that Richard Sennett and Ricky Burdett have set in intriguing motion. Associated with this chapter has been the photographic record created by Dirk Lindner which continues to inspire me. Closer to home the project would not have been possible without the diligent, intelligent support of José de Paiva and in its production to Sarah Blackmore. My partners in practice Robert Kennett and Nick Jackson have been generous in their support and reading of the script. José de Paiva, Tao Sule-DuFour, Eimear Hanratty and Russell Watson have created a number of the drawings for which I am very grateful. Finally for their gracious patience and encouragement I am most indebted to Helen Castle and Merit Claussen.

Contents

Introduction

There are a growing number of remarkable projects reflecting a widening global appetite and audience for architectural adventure. When Frank Gehry's Bilbao Guggenheim Museum opened in 1997, the cherry on the urban renewal cake, it did more at a stroke than the massive infrastructure projects that preceded it, to reinvent the image of that city. Many others have followed suit, calling on the undoubted talents of a battalion of architects who spend as much time in airports as in their offices.

At the same time interest in the city as an urban and social science project has burgeoned with the exponential rate of global urban expansion. Deyan Sudjic's book *The 100 Mile City* (1992) explored the reality of the megacity with a breathtaking pace to mirror its subject. The Urban Age project, centred at the London School of Economics and supported generously by the Deutsche Bank's Alfred Herrhausen Fund, has allowed eminent academics from the fields of law, economics, urban policy, urban design, politics and sociology to circumnavigate the globe to assess the comparative conditions of some of the most influential cities. This work reached a peak of public attention with the Venice Architecture Biennale curated by Ricky Burdett in 2010. The Corderie (the long chain of former naval rope factory buildings where the Biennale's main themed exhibition is held) were packed with comparative statistics, diagnoses of relative infrastructure successes and failures and above all harrowing projections of future growth. It represented an extraordinary effort and contained a huge amount of useful information for the next generation of policy makers, but given that vast space I came away overfed on facts but starved of the qualitative and haptic sense of what makes the world of cities the essential storehouse of human existence. I had contemplated gathering some of the intense urban narrative accumulated in piecemeal fashion by architectural projects that have preoccupied me for a couple of decades into a navigable order, when Helen Castle asked me if I would add *Context* as a title in Wiley's series of books aimed primarily at both students and lecturers involved in the business of architectural education. As a former studio teacher and lecturer, now fully preoccupied by practice, I started to muse on the bridges between the two worlds. There are some things that are difficult and intangible in the school studio, two of the most important being the material and tectonic issues that the building crafts and industry offer to the designer's palette and then additionally the collective nature of architectural design. The latter involves the specialist knowledge of many fields from landscape design to engineering with which architecture forms a synthesising and catalysing voice.

The broad theoretical territory embodied in the book's structure reflects my own wavering between art, architecture and anthropology. Additionally I can trace the roots of my interest in the European city to the lectures and seminars of two of my former teachers: Dalibor Vesely at the Architectural Association in 1978–9 and Kenneth Frampton at the Royal College of Art in 1976–7. Indeed it was Frampton's references to Vesely during a remarkable set of two-hour lectures at the RCA that galvanised me to attend the AA at a time when almost all studios were absorbed by a heated discourse about the contemporary city, fermented by the director of the school, Alvin Boyarsky.

While we can rummage through the history of city planning to ascertain where critical plans emerged, in the case of chapter four the street and the cities under scrutiny, it remains an obvious contradiction to so much muscular architectural effort today that the silent contributors are more often than not anonymous – like the unattributed poet 'unknown'. And yet in their anonymity they have created a framework that is celebrated every day in the most liveable, communicative, entertaining and sophisticated sections of cities on earth.

View from Piazza della Minerva, Rome
Context through the layers of successive epochs: ancient Roman, early Christian, the Baroque and the contemporary. In the foreground is Francesco Borromini's Obelisco della Minerva (1667); in the background, the Pantheon (1st century BC, rebuilt *c* AD 126, with subsequent 17th- and 18th-century additions).

On the question of the future shaping of the city, those archetypes that are as fundamental as eating, sleeping and conversing remain its shared spaces: the streets, the urban block, the square and the public garden. In order to move towards an understanding of the street, the ground on which it is cast seemed an obvious starting point for the first chapter. The making of streets is taken for granted but actually it absorbs a huge quantum of the city dweller's field of vision, constantly dangerous, engaging and subject to all the wear and tear that citizens can muster. Choice of material is resolved by proximity, continuities of tradition and context, and the differences are so clear that is it often possible to locate a place from the traces of its surface alone.

The concern for a perceptual field rather than a focus on particular objects gave rise to the framing of the second chapter, 'Horizon'. In it the vexed question of the city skyline and who determines it is ever present because tall buildings are inescapable – as Roland Barthes's opening quotation in his 1964 essay 'The Eiffel Tower' makes clear: 'Maupassant often lunched at the restaurant in the tower, though he didn't care much for the food: "It's the only place in Paris," he used to say, "where I don't have to see it".'[1] Equally loss of horizon is one of the most terrifying conditions to the living, as the Chilean miners' incarceration made vivid in 2010. One of the most outstanding contributions of 20th-century contemporary architecture has been the structural ability to manipulate the datum and thus to create multiple horizons, which is developed through some fine precedents. The spatial and cultural layering that design can engender lies at the heart of the third chapter, titled 'Simultaneity': every society holds different nuances to these proximities, and their combinations are at work at every scale from the room to the make-up of the city itself. The chapter I hope serves as an introduction to one of the most useful ways of thinking about design beyond the object. The final chapter, 'Artifice', is structured around the paradoxical character of the urban public garden as a place of play and encounter.

The restorative power of nature drawn through artifice into the urban landscape has created places of real communicative power that symbolise the particularity and fragility of context as an essential part of human habitation.

References

1. Roland Barthes, 'The Eiffel Tower' [1964], in *The Eiffel Tower and Other Mythologies*, translated by R Howard, University of California Press (Berkeley, Los Angeles and London), 1997, p 3.

Pavement

Architecture differs from the other visual and performance-based arts in one fundamental respect: its interdependence on the ground upon which it sits. Clearly, sculpture, in its most monumental and public manifestation, shares with architecture its particularity of place; while at the other end of the spectrum, temporary art structures or installations – like nomadic tents, which can also be architectural – have more in common with the transience of performance and the passing of a musical note.

The grounded quality of architecture can also render it a significant meeting point for the specific historical and geological moment. In the ancient act of founding, the first incision of the plough marks out the boundaries of a city, the furrow peeling back the crust of the seasons to reveal the bedrock of time on which a defensive wall is erected and the future incubated.

The complex cultural interdependence of the surface and geological substance of the ground is immediately apparent in the 'fervour' of wine- or cheesemakers for their local *terroir*. Like a discussion of the specificity of the

Boyle Family, *Holland Park Avenue Study, London Series*, 1967 and *Cobbles Study, Lorrypark Series*, 1976
Boyle Family's 'Journey to the Surface of the Earth' raised the pavement through their urban taxidermy of the everyday, to the status of high culture. Shown here is part of a display of their work at the Scottish National Gallery of Modern Art, Edinburgh in 2003.

ecosystems that miraculously deliver the bacterial bloom on the skin of a grape, the stones that make up the pavements we walk on have their own particular qualities that, when combined with the traditions of laying down, create an instantly recognisable texture, colour and scale – an indelible link to a particular context.

Latent Common Ground

We tend to take pavements for granted. In fact, they are so much a part of the ritual of daily life that it is as sources of disruption that they first come to mind: the seemingly endless round of upheavals that are caused by the repairing of pipes, threading of new cables, or the re-laying of so often inadequately repaired surfaces. Paradoxically, they bear the earliest and the most recent traces of habitation: on the one hand, the grid of streets that make up towns and cities is the most permanent of topographical features (ironically becoming more so as the ground beneath fills with an ever-increasingly complex maze of services); on the other hand, the rituals of renewal, the gathering of detritus and debris embodied in street cleaning are a litmus test of municipal order, the economics of taxation and social habit. I was first consciously struck by this extreme polarity in the work of the artists Boyle Family. Their exhibition 'Journey to the Surface of the Earth' at London's Serpentine Gallery in the early summer of 1975 depicted, with sharp-focused super-realism and a taxidermic instinct for preservation, the unexpected dislocation of sections of the pavement surfaces on to the gallery wall. The permanence of a kerb stone or a gulley was juxtaposed with the immediacy of the jettisoned and weather-blown human traces – cigarette butts, dust and paper – located by the chance encounter of a dart thrown at a city map.

Coincidentally, over time, gathering thoughts for seminars, for precedent studies and just musing on different settings, I became aware that my own pre-digital 35mm-film archive contained a series of photographs, taken inadvertently in the process of 'winding on' the film into the camera, which were often images of pavements. They became for me the equivalent of a scientist's Petri dish, for it becomes strikingly clear that so much that is particular to a place is embodied in its pavements, geology, modules, textures and habits. This chapter sets out to explore through examples the hidden depths of this latent common ground. Whether negotiated with the tapping antennae of the blind, the jogger's air-cushioned soles, or a child's running feet, we all share the continuous appraisal of what is at the next instant to be found underfoot. We are able to ascertain in a calibration of extraordinary finesse and agility, the paving stone's qualities: its firmness, slipperiness, evenness or even its inclination – something that has continued to elude the best efforts of robotics. For that is what pavements are about: movement and temporality.

Paving the Sacred, Profane and Political

The other dimension that is provocatively striking is the way that pavements, while embodying both the everyday and most seemingly mundane rituals of life, have also led to some of the most sophisticated representations of cosmological order. Pavements provide evidence of political and cultural will.

This can be autocratic as in the ubiquitous homogeneity of the brick surfaces of the Imperial Palace in the Forbidden City of Beijing, or the concrete *Autobahnen* of the Third Reich; mercantile as in the meeting of sea and desert in the Gulf States and the great trading routes of the Silk Road and salt roads; ceremonial as in the entry at London Bridge to the City of London (see the following section of this chapter); sacred as in the pilgrim routes of Europe and the processional way followed for millennia in a city like Enna in Sicily; or bridge the shared territories of the sacred and the secular as in the streets of Bhuleshwar in Mumbai.

Close-up photographs of pavements
Left to right: Henrietta Street, Dublin, Ireland, vestiges of grandeur and dereliction; monumental interlocking slabs of the Corso di Porta Ticinese, Milan, Italy; pavement detail of the Chiado, Lisbon, Portugal; reordered field stones, setts and precast paths at the Stortorget, Kalmar, Sweden; Stolpersteine, Martin-Luther-King-Platz, Hamburg, Germany; water's edge at San Giorgio Maggiore, Venice, Italy; detail of the *opus sectile* work of the Cosmati sanctuary pavement, Westminster Abbey, London; Proconnesian marble slabs forming the floor, a frozen sea, in the Hagia Sophia, Istanbul, Turkey.

The basic unit of paving, the stone, provides it with a universal and timeless quality, whether it is a trail staking out a route or a monument marking a deceased life. It is this aspect that is explored in the final section of this chapter, regarding memory, through the pilgrim passage around the sacred water basin of Banganga Tank in India and the Stolpersteine project by artist Gunter Demnig, which erects cobblestone-sized memorials to individual victims of the Nazis.

While the *Autobahnen*, trading and pilgrimage routes stretch the spatial boundaries of the citizen's right of passage as a pedestrian into the realm of travel over long homogeneous and repetitive surfaces that connect urban centres, the particularity of the paving of a sacred space combines a reverie on the ecstatic vertical contemplation of earth and sky. This culminates in the floorscapes of public buildings where meditation on surfaces becomes a key to temporal reflection – geological in the materiality of stone, historical through geometric arrangement, and human through the individual and the drama of ritual. This is highlighted in the sea-like expanse of the Proconnesian marble floor in the nave of the Hagia Sofia in Istanbul (see the section of

this chapter on 'Sacred Surfaces'). The pavement, or *der Bürgersteig* (literally 'citizens' way'), is therefore much more about the individual's liberty to see and be seen, to participate in the daily drama of the city, than about circulation, security and segregation. For Álvaro Siza, restoring the pavement of Lisbon's Chiado district (see 'Lisbon's Carpet' section of this chapter) was also an essential first step in revitalising the area after a fire in 1988. An emphasis on the routine aspects of the everyday points to the difference between the Situationists' 'society of the spectacle',[1] or the tourists' fleeting appetite, and the daily round of working, learning, playing and ageing in the unfolding cycles of politics and cultural change from the citizen's point of view. Public space is not a given that naturally evolves; it often has to be reasserted and redefined – most recently in order to fend off the dominance of the car. This is demonstrated in the successful regeneration and pedestrianisation of Stortorget, the 17th-century main square of Kalmar in Sweden, by Caruso St John Architects and artist Eva Löfdahl (see 'Field of Stones, Kalmar' section of this chapter). The citizens' pavement as opposed to the gated realm is also an important test of society's inclusiveness. Like a section of Giambattista Nolli's 1748 plan of Rome or the classical city, how far the stain of public access penetrates the body of the city suggests a culture's vitality and common ground. The artificiality of a corporate section of the city, like Broadgate or Canary Wharf in London, is made clear when these boundaries are challenged.

London Bridge

Closed doors and chain-link fencing are not the only protagonists in the shifting sands of the politics of the pavement; borders, for instance – those

of ownership as in the 'estates' of London or boroughs – play their part, as does the mind-set of the traffic engineer. The results for the citizen can be catastrophic, as at the edge of London Bridge. The bridge, a magnet for congestion and confusion, is the *raison d'être* of London. It was used as a crossing as early as Neolithic times (the 9th century BC). Further east than other ancient fords, it was the point of a natural causeway over the southern marshes leading across the river to the rise now known as Cornhill. When the Romans invaded, they layered their own structures here by initially building a temporary military pontoon and then replacing it with the first permanent, timber-piled bridge; in the ensuing centuries, it fell into disrepair, prey to the vicissitudes of Saxon and Danish squabbling. It was only following the Norman invasion of 1066 that the bridge was rebuilt. Henry II (1133–1189) created a monastic guild, the 'Brethren of the Bridge', to oversee all work on the timber bridge; and in 1176, Peter de Colechurch, a priest and head of the Brethren, began building the first stone bridge across the Thames, funded by a wool tax. This had a chapel dedicated to Thomas Becket at its centre, 19 arches, a drawbridge, and defensive gatehouses at each end. By Tudor times, the bridge had some two hundred buildings rising up to seven stories with a two-lane, 3.7-metre- (12-foot-) wide road tunnelling beneath – grinding, smoking and shitting like a Lilliputian nightmare. At its head, the tousled southern gateway was crowned by some thirty tarred traitors' heads, so vividly displayed in Claes Janszoon Visscher's 1616 *View of London from South Bank*.

London Bridge, Duke Hill Street and Tooley Street, Southwark: pre-existing site, London, 1996
As found in 1996, two photo collages of the site before the interventions. Top image to the left, London Bridge, and to the right, Duke Hill Street. The concrete balustrade to the ramp which leads to London Bridge Station acts as a defensive wall insulating commuters from the 'Borough'. The City of London Corporation owns the land demarcated by the paving slabs at the centre, Southwark the rest.

Though the relationship between the bridge and the tightly defined City of London are all clear in Visscher's etching, which looks towards the City from the South Bank, it was paradoxically the very existence of the City's physical borders – defined by the old Roman walls and the Thames – that first provided a catalyst for development on the opposite bank and the erosion of the significance of this route and its clear boundaries. Since the medieval period, the proximity of the South Bank to the City made it a popular site of entertainment and illegal activities, such as brothels and gaming exchanges, safely outside and beyond the City's jurisdiction. In the Elizabethan era, Shakespeare made Southwark the location for the Globe theatre; and

Eric Parry Architects, Southwark Gateway, London, 1997–9: needle
The stone needle, the trajectory of which marks the historic threshold to London, is fabricated of 25 keyed blocks of Portland stone that are post-tensioned to act as one element with a stepped base, which is an invitation or gateway southwards to Southwark.

during the Restoration in the mid-17th century, the Vauxhall Pleasure Gardens, which Samuel Pepys famously recorded visiting in his diaries, were established on the south bank of the Thames at Kennington. With industrialisation in the 18th and 19th centuries, commercial activities also intensified south of the river, and it became a magnet for industries that were deemed undesirable

within the confines of the City's walls: noxious tanning, hatmaking, brewing, shipbuilding and the docks.

By the 18th century, the stone medieval bridge – now six hundred years old – had become a major source of congestion for road and river traffic alike.

Eric Parry Architects, Southwark Gateway, London, 1997–9: light pavement
The granite remains of one arch of John Rennie's 19th-century bridge are encapsulated within the structure of its 1973 replacement. The lost river edge is evoked through the LED light display held in cast-iron frames within in-situ washed aggregate concrete.

Claes Janszoon Visscher, *View of London from South Bank*, 1616
This etching of the ever fascinating 17th-century panorama of London offers a vivid depiction of the South Bank, the city and the bridge – almost always a site of change and construction to the present.

Interim measures were adopted, such as southbound carts and carriages being required to drive on the left-hand side and northbound vehicles on the right; and the demolition of all houses and shops on the bridge. In 1799, a competition was launched for a new design for London Bridge. Despite a field that included Thomas Telford, the Scottish engineer John Rennie (1761–1821) won with a proposal for a five-arched bridge that was adopted and eventually completed 32 years later under the supervision of his son. (It was Rennie's bridge that was famously sold in 1963 to the American tycoon Robert McCulloch, who allegedly mistook it for Tower Bridge; it has now been replaced by a 1973 bridge designed by Lord Holford.) The new bridge was built 30 metres (100 feet) to the west of the fabled medieval bridge, and the most expensive part of the project was the construction of the new approach roads to north and south. To either side of the bridge the embankment was cleared locally for the construction and reconstruction of subsequent bridge improvements watched over by the City of London with its economic interests in an uninterrupted flow of commerce. The South Bank, cut off from its hinterland by the acreage of railway-supporting brick vaults, was characterised by a comb of wharves perpendicular to the river's edge fed by small boats and the community of boatmen so vividly described by Charles Dickens in the opening chapters of *Our Mutual Friend* (1864–5).[2] The railway marked the exponential rise of pedestrians dutifully making a daily commute to the City possible. TS Eliot's seminal poem *The Waste Land*, first published in 1922, has London Bridge woven into its five sections and is a topography

that Eliot knew all too well, working as he did for eight years at Lloyds Bank after teaching and prior to his editorship at Faber and Faber. He explored the bridge at its most purgatorial in lines 60–69 in the first section of the poem, 'The Burial of the Dead', famously saying of the flow of commuters making their morning crossing: 'I had not thought death had undone so many.'[3]

Eliot's *The Waste Land* epitomises in its dark mood the general state of inertia of Southwark's South Bank until the mid-1990s: the hulk of the redundant power station; the dereliction of open sites like Potters Fields; the vast acreage of Victorian brick vaults supporting the railway infrastructure. Into this vacuum, just as property investors began to rediscover the area and it started to attract new residents, stepped the regeneration unit at the London Borough of Southwark, headed by Fred Manson who, wary of another grand urban masterplan, seeded through a competitive process a series of small-scale interventions of improved public realm. Under the broad title 'Future Southwark', an exhibition of the proposals was held in 1996 in a disused carwash shed (since demolished to make way for Crossrail). The artist Michael Craig-Martin painted a giant-scale Anglepoise lamp, the first of his numerous installation wall paintings, to signal the show on the street.

With hindsight, this exhibition was the catalyst for the trajectory of engagement with urban landscape design for several now well-known London practices. Muf proposed a scheme for Southwark Street called Groundswell. East, working in Borough High Street, proposed a repairing scheme including terrazzo threshold slabs, many of which were implemented. Florian Beigel and the Architecture Research Unit of what was then the University of North London (now London Metropolitan University) proposed linkages from Southwark Street to the southern open space of the power station which became the planning policy for the redevelopment of St Christopher's House. Patel Taylor proposed landscaping and connections to the north of the power station. All these practices have gone on to contribute internationally recognised public realm improvement schemes in London, which have been a notable contribution to a wider cultural debate.

Our contribution as the architects for this site was a study of the abject state of Colechurch House, a building owned by the Bridge House Estates (a charitable trust belonging to the City of London Corporation and a throwback to the 12th-century Brethren of the Bridge). The building straddles the conduit for human traffic from London Bridge station onto London Bridge while insulating them from the London Borough of Southwark to the south.

Gabriel Bodenehr, *Lisabon oder Olyssipo*, c 1700–58
Based on a 16th-century original, this engraving shows Lisbon as the image of organic urban growth in the alluvial valley between the higher ground before the earthquake of 1755.

This messy hit-and-miss picture of unrequited public realm ambitions evoked by London Bridge in which public infrastructure is patched up and dusted down, and only replaced when needs absolutely must, is typical of the way London has stumbled into existence free of any absolute or coherent planning force. In this respect the city form of Lisbon provides a stark contrast, having being reconstructed after the earthquake of 1755 and the fire of 1988. The continuity of its pavements remains a haunting presence.

Lisbon's Carpet

Watching a group of workmen lay a section of Lisbon pavement is, as Álvaro Siza has pointed out, like observing a craft tradition passed down continuously from generation to generation from at least Roman times – let us say therefore a couple of thousand years![4] The pavement is in Lisbon's historic Chiado district, an area that was destroyed by the fire of 1988 and has been reconstructed under Siza's direction. The paving has a characteristic tessellated form: hard white limestone cubes are bordered and patterned with black basalt cubes of a similar size. Both the limestone and basalt are local to the Lisbon area; geologically Portugal can be divided around its central latitude between the granite-based north and the limestone and marble south. Siza recalls:

> In the Chiado I insisted in using the same pavement (granite cubes in the roads and traditional mosaics in the pedestrian walks) and I fought to maintain motorcar traffic in the whole area (which I didn't get completely), to guarantee continuity with most of the other streets in Baixa. This because I see with reserve the tendency to divide vehicle and pedestrian traffic – with some exceptions, of course. In this issue my favorite city is Naples, where everything is mixed and seems somehow chaotic ... but there are no accidents and the whole city is full of life.[5]

Trafficked streets traditionally are made from a larger module of the dark stone, but between kerbstones and stepped ramp edging all the paved surfaces flow sometimes across steep topography or negotiating abrupt changes in direction – an excellent solution for this historic city built across a hilly landscape and a deep alluvial valley where the downtown came to develop. The pavements unify and create a mental image like the ordering of a narrative as strong as those of the *azulejo*, the Portuguese tradition of painted tin-glazed ceramic wall tiles, which were imported from Flanders in the 16th century and later exported to the Indies. Found on the exteriors and interiors of domestic and public buildings, they often chronicle scenes from hagiography and Portuguese history.

But to return to those workmen: a group of four or five will be required to work on a relatively small area, if a complex border is required, such as the sign or number for an adjacent threshold. A guiding template is cut in plastic sheeting. At the centre, a hand picks out an appropriate-sized stone cube from a pile, delivered within arm's reach, and it is placed slightly raised and snugly close to its neighbours in a fine granular substrate. The pavers tap out a continuous light rhythm with their steel-headed hammers against the hard stones of the laid surface. It is a rhythm that is punctuated by a duller tone as the new stone finds its pitch and place. This quiet melody is very much part of the streetscape, a sign of continuous repair and maintenance – the city at work. The other response that the small module allows is the adjustment to local movement of the earth beneath the roads and buildings.

Despite the adjustment of traditional building techniques to Lisbon's dramatic topography and the looming threat of a seism, nothing could have prepared Lisbon for the catastrophe of All Saints' Day 1755. Three earthquakes struck: the first during morning mass. The event gripped Enlightenment Europe and one of its most important figures, Voltaire, wrote an epic poem *On the Lisbon Disaster (or: An Examination of the Axiom 'All is Well')*, and playing on his imagination it formed a central section to the adventures of Candide in his novel of the same name, in which the eponymous hero after escaping the ravages finds himself in the part of the city of Lisbon 'still weeping over the death of their benefactor. Candide and Pangloss had hardly set foot in the town when they suddenly felt the earth shaking beneath their feet. The sea seethed in the port, wrecking the ships anchored there, and whirls of fire and ash covered the streets and the squares. Houses collapsed, roofs caving in on crumbling foundations.'[6] The devastation was most fierce in the alluvial plane running evenly towards the Tagus between two hills; to the east the concentric and irregular street pattern descending like a three-dimensional image from the Castelo de São Jorge; to the west the 16th-century grid of the Bairro Alto.

The 18th-century reconstruction proceeded under the autocratic direction of the remarkably energetic and gifted Sebastião José de Carvalho e Melo –

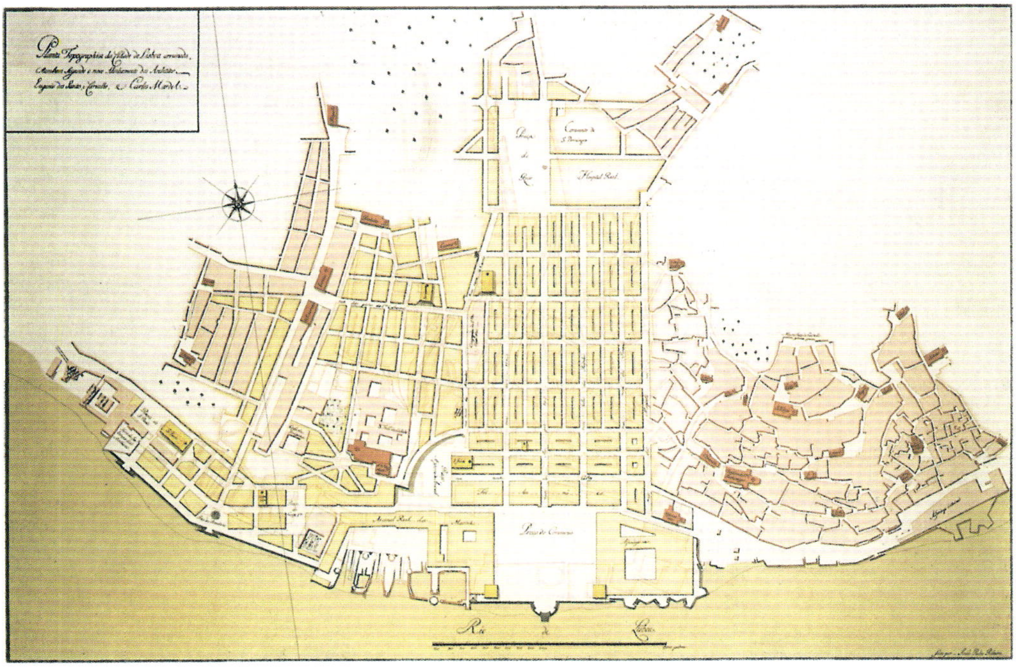

Eugénio dos Santos and Carlos Mardel, *Planta Topographica da Cidade de Lisboa*, 1758
This 1947 lithograph shows the chosen scheme of planned rebuilding of the gridded Baixa district of 1758, three years after the devastation: an Enlightenment essay in urban design in response to Voltaire's paradoxical statement 'All is well'.

the future Marquis of Pombal, who had eleven years earlier returned from a five-year ambassadorial posting in England, where he would have witnessed from his home in Golden Square, London, the 17th-century squares of Lincoln's Inn Fields, Covent Garden and St James's Square, but also the concurrent building boom of the Hanoverian ascension including St George Street and Hanover Square.

Following the havoc wreaked by the earthquake, he commissioned a detailed topographical survey, forbade any immediate rebuilding, and over the period of a year commissioned five alternative proposals. The chosen proposal by Eugénio dos Santos and Carlos Mardel, built out over the next century and a half, was startlingly closely adhered to, including the urban block, number of storeys, walling and window detailing, balconies, roofs and a very innovative construction methodology *a 'jaula' pombalina*,[7] essentially a sophisticated balloon-framed timber skeleton that would remain

Aerial photograph of Baixa-Chiado, Lisbon, 1988
A photograph of the Baixa-Chiado district taken after the fire, the aftermath of which is clearly visible in the centre left margin. Of note, the built mirror of the Santos/Mardel plan of 1758

intact if the outer stone skin collapsed in an earthquake, without disturbing the adjacent building – this last concern also helping to determine the width of streets. The district has come to be known as the Baixa, and its light-honed limestone paving reflects the sky and distant water by day, lightening the tones of the stone walls at their junction, and reflects by night the life of public ground-floor interiors.

When the Chiado district bordering the western edge of the Baixa was engulfed in fire on 25 August 1988, a collective groan of despair, as soul-searching as Voltaire's, could be felt. A significant setting of Portuguese 19th- and 20th-century literary and artistic culture vaporised. In truth the area had lost its shine in recent years and the fact that the fire burnt undeterred was the result of many of the upper floors of the buildings being used purely for paper and archival storage.

Almost a quarter of a century after the fire, the Chiado is rebuilt. It is again alive with a dense mix of uses. There are new urban courts and passages, and the Baixa-Chiado Metro Station, a transport interchange on the scale of the ancient Baths of Caracalla in Rome. This new hub, reconnecting the city, was envisaged by Álvaro Siza early on in the district's reconstruction. In the immediate aftermath of the tragedy the city council simply turned to Siza for guidance, as Jorge Sampaio, the then Mayor of Lisbon, and latterly President of Portugal, recalled it:

> As Mayor, I was responsible for the recovery process of a zone that represents the heart of the city … one of the most beautiful sites in the world. … All the difficulties and efforts were compensated for by the privilege and immediate delight of my permanent contact with Professor Álvaro Siza. Evidently, we had agreements and disagreements, but we kept up a stimulating debate that was so enriching for me that it became one of my most vivid memories of public life.[8]

These words condense what the following chapters might otherwise struggle to do by highlighting the intensity and importance of a project that, through its pavements, defines new space and routes, recasting an urban quarter with a modesty that is surprising from the hand of the great master of form. As Siza's public access plan for Chiado illustrates, the reconstruction of more than twenty buildings is contained within three blocks: A, B and C. Block A contains a new heart, an open patio. This is perched between the 12.5-metre (41-foot) difference in level of the Rua Ivens to the west and the Rua Nova do

Almada, and lying directly over the new underground pedestrian tunnel that emerges under Block C in the Rua do Crucifixo, 22 metres (72 feet) below the level of Rua Ivens. Notable but tangential to the discussion of pavements is the entirely rebuilt Castro & Melo building at 89 to 101 Rua Nova do Almada, a mixed-use urban building of breathtakingly simple elegance in its planning and detailing. Block C contains the Chiado department store, topped by a new hotel, and the reworking of the interior of the late 19th-century Grandella department store. Another opportunity was offered by the reconstruction of Block B whose width spreads from its southern elevation facing the Rua Garrett, along the western elevation facing the Calçada do Sacramento, and the east-facing elevation along Rua do Carmo. Siza's early sketch of March 1989 shows the intuition, later reinforced by historical evidence, of the potential of a new ramped pedestrian spine leading from the epicentre of the district at the junction of the three blocks to the skeletal shattered ruins of the Convento do Carmo embodying the memory of 1755.

Álvaro Siza, Plan of Public Access, Chiado, Lisbon, 1989
From within and between the renewed buildings, a network of passages, courts and stair re-establish the previously choked secondary routes of the public realm.

Key

Buildings affected by the fire

Entirely destroyed

Partially destroyed

Integrated in the affected area

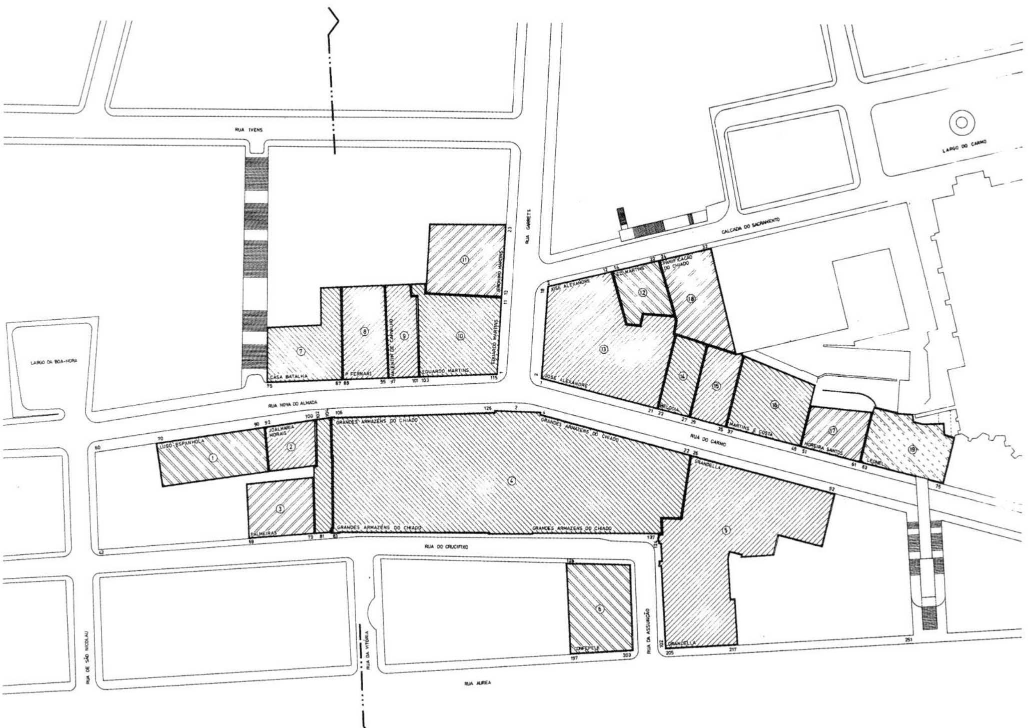

At the head of the new ramp, the passage bifurcates along the southern wall of the monastery west to the finely proportioned square Largo do Carmo and east to the bridge and belvedere of the Santa Justa lift. The comparison with the downtown plan before the fire reinforces the perception that the Chiado was in a state of relative decay, with dwellings almost eliminated; the remarkable reworking of the buildings has seen rejuvenation with a good percentage of housing mixed with other uses, around the wonderfully inventive sets of block interiors, patios and passages. The history and topography that appear so restrictive have through the calamity of the fire become an opportunity to reactivate the hierarchy of the urban pavement and interconnecting tissue. In Siza's words:

> The undulation of the hills opens up like a carpet that someone has stretched out, a dense pattern, stones from which great but serenely simplistic buildings emerge, large terraces, supporting walls covered in gladioli; it opens out, follows the river, as if in breath taking 'Traveling'. Your gaze is lost at sea, the horizon trembles.[9]

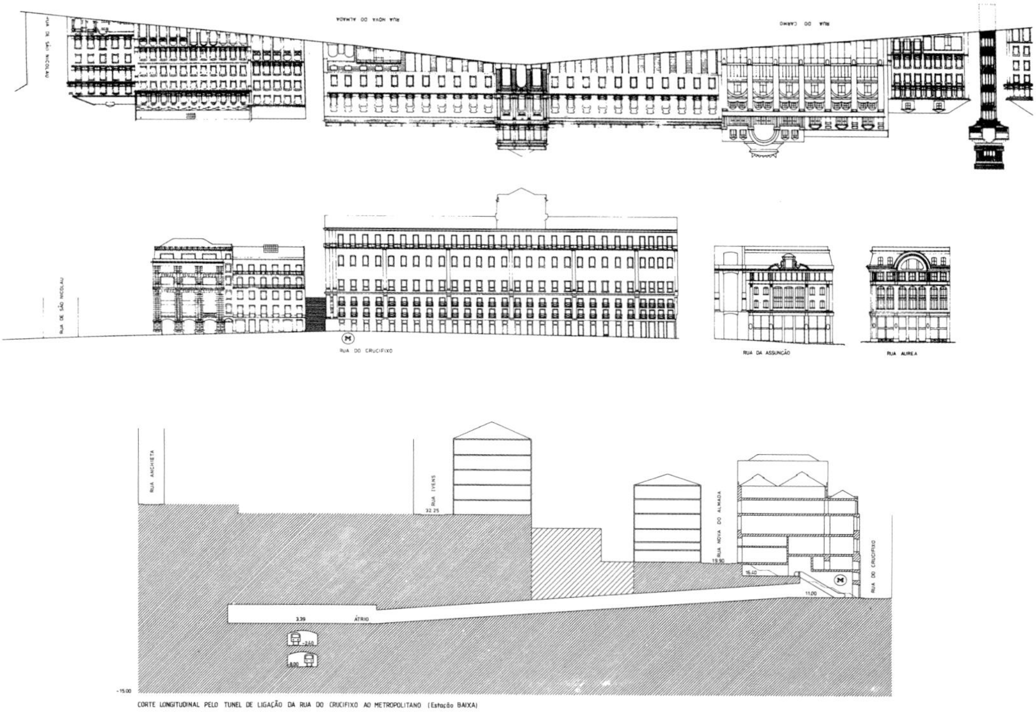

Álvaro Siza, Elevations of Rua do Carmo and Rua Nova do Almada, Chiado, Lisbon, 1989
The striking surface topography in plan and section is reinforced by the new infrastructure of the underground station set close by the 19th-century lift tower.

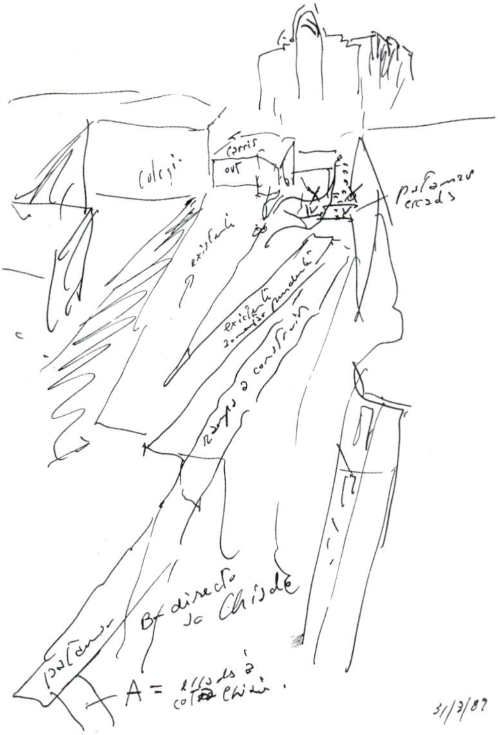

Field of Stones, Kalmar

After the historical and topographical excitement of Lisbon and London, the reordered surface of Stortorget, the main square of the small city of Kalmar in southeast Sweden, stands out for its stark simplicity. Far removed from the scrutiny of a capital city, Kalmar lies on the Swedish Baltic seaboard. Founded around the year 1200, it is one of the country's oldest cities, having grown out of close trading links with the Hanseatic League: the confederation of merchant guilds and market towns that dominated and protected trade from the Late Middle Ages in Northern Germany and the Baltic. Located near the Danish border, Kalmar became strategically important in the 16th and 17th centuries during the Swedish–Danish Kalmar Wars, but this military focus gave way to shipping as the border was permanently settled south. Kalmar's massive defensive castle, with its accumulation of square towers, corner knuckles and enfilades of grand rooms ranged around a central court, was host to the original city around its curtilage.

Georges Demaye, Grandella department store, Chiado, Lisbon, 1907
Photograph of the Grandella department store looking southwards up the Rua do Carmo, c 1940, showing the paving system of tessellated blocks – larger for vehicles, smaller for pedestrians – capable of gymnastic topographical manipulation.

Álvaro Siza, study of the access landings to Carmo, Chiado, Lisbon, 1989
The poetic intent on of Siza's early sketch of the re-establishment of the route to the Carmo, the living skeleton reminder of 1755 at the heart of his Chiado proposals.

In 1639 the Swedish council of the realm decided that the entire city should be moved from its vulnerable position to the unpopulated island of Kvarnholmen. It was at this stage that Stortorget, the main square, was conceived as a 98-by-107-meter (320-by-350-foot) opening in the grid of the urban block: a space that was then to be dominated by the autonomous mass of Nicodemus Tessin the Elder's Baroque cathedral, begun in 1660, on a base of cyclopean-scale masonry rising out of the surface of the square. The mass of the church, to this day, effectively overshadows half of the square with its south portal centred on the axis of the square, and a line that bisects the square north to south passing just south of the portal steps. The remainder of the square, which was originally used as a space for military drills, the weekly market and public meetings, and as an important source for water as the site of the city's main well, is significantly placed on the axis of the church and Storgatan, the city's main street. This road crosses the public double-squared rectangle at approximately the centre of its shorter side. By the end of the 20th century, this road had come to dominate the square. When, in 1998, the Kalmar County Museum published a document tracing the metamorphosis of the square's surface, they entitled it *Stortorget, från brunn till P-mätare* (*Main Square, from Well to Parking Metre*).[10] Four plans, reconstructing the square's surfaces in 1800, 1900, 1920 and 1940 respectively, describe the progressive formalisation of the segregation of pedestrian and vehicular movement. This point is evocatively illustrated in an etching of Stortorget by Nils-Isak

Aerial photograph of Kvarnholmen, Sweden, 2005
The Stortorget lies at the centre of Kvarnholmen, planned in the 1600s and executed in full.

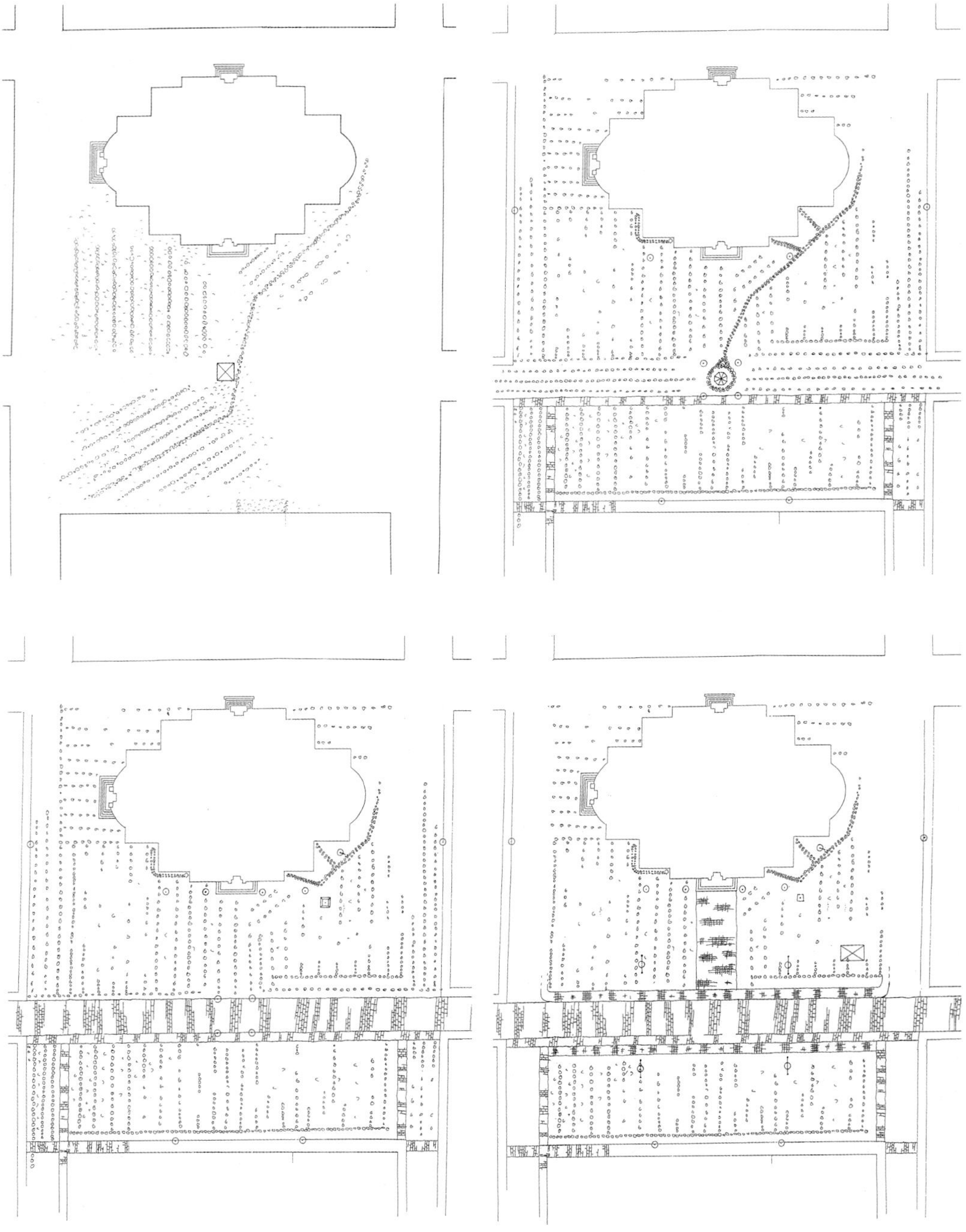

Nicodemus Tessin the Elder, Kalmar Cathedral, Kvarnholmen, begun 1660
An aerial photograph taken in 1920, showing Nicodemus Tessin the Elder's monumental Baroque cathedral dominating the square.

Löfgren dating back to 1837. The square's original surfacing resonated with the place in its use of available material and its unselfconsciousness. The stones that made up the original surface are 'field stones', a geological mix of predominantly granite pebbles and boulders ground to a smooth finish by the progresses and recessions of the Ice Age, stacked into dry-stone walling and providing the raw material to make the streets and squares of the Baroque city over centuries. These variegated stones have been laid, shifted and re-laid, and are easily distinguished from the homogeneity of the later cut-granite street paving. The field stone surface was evidently laid by first creating parallel level rows of larger stones, called line stones, and infilling the space between with smaller stones to create a level surface throughout.

Richard Edlund and Örjan Molander, drawings from *Stortorget, från brunn till P-mätare*, Kalmar Läns Museum (Kalmar), 1998
Drawings of the surface materials of the square in 1800, 1900, 1920 and 1940 (right to left, top to bottom) showing the 'line stones' used to establish the levels of parallel lines and the surfaces in between, a progression that ended in the domination of the car.

The photographic documentation of the square preceding its renovation by Caruso St John Architects and Eva Löfdahl in 2002 shows the continuous process of segregation of the public space in detail: raised kerbs defining pedestrian areas, bollards, bicycle racks, flagpoles, folk light fitting and ugly signage. In short, it represented that all too typical relapse into half measures that are universally taken for granted as acceptable. An inspired and crucial part of the success of the built project was the mutually supportive relationship between the selected design team of artist and architects. An interest in architecture was kindled by a government directive demanding that the Swedish Arts Council's remit for the commission include the 'public environment'. The scheme, which was well developed by the time that the team entered the international competition for the square's design in 1999, broadly meant that the architects took responsibility for the surface of

Nils-Isak Löfgren, *Stortorget, Kalmar*, 1837
Löfgren's etching of the Stortorget suggests a continuous homogeneous stage upon which the civic participants create a foreground and hinterland.

the square, and the artist Eva Löfdahl, the imaginary space above and the chthonic space below this surface. Their intense relationship is evoked in Löfdahl's words:

> our correspondence relating to Stortorget is plentiful. It spans five years and is intense at times, with several exchanges a day .... Naturally it contains a great deal of practical information ... but the rest is just as significant. Our sessions in Kalmar were packed with presentations and meetings with representatives. Afterwards we were often too tired to speak. ... During the periods when not much was happening, we all digressed into other ideas and tasks. We then needed to repeat what had already been discussed, to 're-establish the energy' over and over again.[11]

In the final project, this manifested itself in the artist devising the choreography and latent meaning for the installation of new wells or

Eva Löfdahl and Caruso St John Architects, regeneration of Stortorget, Kalmar, Sweden, 2003: detail of pavement
Detail of the 'line stones' and infilling field stones with the shadow of one of the cathedral's four lantern-topped towers.

sound chambers and stainless-steel lighting masts, which effectively mediate the earth, sky and nearby water; while the almost abstract composition of the plan generated by the presence of buildings, traces of movement and the craftsmanship of the past, was engendered by the architects' idea of a collage of textures, which responds to the passing of people and the moving shadows of the buildings and masts. Taking the past as an inspiration, Löfdahl has rekindled a hauntingly trapped connection to the underworld with her sound chambers that speak to the passer-by coming in and passing out of auditory focus through the freedom of movement in the social world. The stainless-steel masts, topped by hand-blown red glass domed cylinders, act by night as a loose web whose disconnection from the orthogonal surface order are like the inaccessible jewels of a paradisiacal sphere.

The admirably refined drawing of the surface, as completed, culminated in a process that was begun by Caruso St John during the competition, of creating almost rug-dimensioned drawings. It is interesting that Stortorget runs counter to the urban grain of streets by being represented as an independent square. The traces of the positions of entry and exit roads are the vestigial inflections of the kerb stones forming the only framing device at the perimeter of the space. Four finely proportioned rectangles reminiscent of

Eva Löfdahl and Caruso St John Architects, regeneration of Stortorget, Kalmar, Sweden, 2003: view from Kalmar Cathedral
The reordering of the surface area (98 by 107 metres (320 by 350 feet)) involved the reuse of field stones; large and small cobblestones; precast concrete slabs; six 12-metre- (40-foot-) tall stainless-steel masts topped by hand-blown glass lanterns; five wells with precast lids; and cast-iron bollards.

Eva Löfdahl and Caruso St John Architects, regeneration of Stortorget, Kalmar, Sweden, 2003: detail of pavement
The 1.5-metre- (5-foot-) diameter precast covers of the artist Eva Löfdahl's sound chambers establish a link to a chthonic underworld.

constructivist compositional exercises are described as 'clearings', places that acknowledge the square's other major buildings. These are made of granite setts of cobblestone pavement known colloquially as *kullersten*, of a regular width that have been skilfully re-laid using the material that made up the road surface introduced in the early 20th century. The treatment given to the stone pavement was intended to reflect the nature of its geological and fossil material, namely the so-called 'cat skulls' (*kattskallar*), a type of fossil almost only found on the Swedish island of Gotland. The lightness and smoothness creates a sharp contrast with the older irregularity of the field stone surface that has been repaired and expanded as the principal body of the square. The main axis through the square, now marked as a pedestrian width, is formed by large precast slabs that create another scaling, larger than a single pace, introducing a miniature pattern not unlike the field stones in the washed and exposed granite aggregate. These panels have also a subtle shift in width and direction that acknowledges the primary entry and the change of axiality leading to the south porch of the cathedral. Altogether it is a very satisfying combination of modesty – acknowledging the history of the place – and clarity of purpose. In Adam Caruso's words:

> Without the freedom to choose material or technique this project is completely about form and largely about shifting existing material. It is energy neutral in a way that Beuys and Smithson might have approved of.[12]

What is clear is that the re-imagination of Stortorget by Caruso St John and Löfdahl required the breadth of vision of large-scale land art, such as Joseph Beuys's *7000 Oaks – City Forestation Instead of City Administration*, presented at Documenta 7 in Kassel (1982), or Robert Smithson's *Spiral Jetty* (1970). Paradoxically, though, as Caruso has pointed out through the complementary juxtaposition of the new and the original, a cycle of intervention was cleansed. It thus raised the ire of antiquarians who saw the erasure as arrogant; in Caruso's words: 'After long and philosophical discussions, formal coherence was chosen over the ambiguity of history.'[13]

It is with the injection of a certain element of 'sparkle' in the scheme that a wonderful balance of nature, place and artifice is achieved in this exemplary project. This is attained by the needle-like, stainless-steel light ports with their worked surfaces and the sharpness of their gnomon-like shadows cast over the new and old surfaces; and by the highly polished circular precast and stainless-steel grille well covers that are the mouthpieces of a chthonic underworld.

Sacred Surfaces

The composition and scale of pavements, the resonance of their materiality and their capacity to transcend the everyday are most evident historically in sacred spaces. In this penultimate section of this chapter, the extremes of relatively undifferentiated material in the marvellous paving of the Hagia Sophia in Istanbul (532–7) are investigated, at one end of the spectrum, and at the other, the complex material and geometric symbolism of the Cosmati Pavement (1238) in Westminster Abbey.

At the turn of the 20th century, the influential Arts and Crafts architect WR Lethaby (1857–1931) inspired a group of young likeminded enthusiasts to explore the architecture of the early Christian church in the Eastern Roman Empire through his research and writings on iconography and cosmology and specifically his monograph on the Hagia Sophia or Sancta Sophia.[14] Robert Weir Schultz and Sidney Howard Barnsley, for instance, went on to write *The Monastery of Saint Luke of Stiris, in Phocis, and the Dependent Monastery of Saint Nicolas in the Fields near Skripou in Boeotia* (published in 1901).

These further studies gave rise to a number of neo-Byzantine buildings, most prominently Westminster Cathedral (1903) by John Francis Bentley (1839–1902) with a chapel by Robert Weir Schultz (1860–1951), but also at a smaller scale the Church of the Holy Wisdom at Lower Kingswood, Surrey (1891) by Sidney Barnsley (1865–1926), which is now less well known than it ought to be. Adopting the form of a Roman basilica with a central apse,

Eric Parry Architects, axonometric section of the Hagia Sophia, Constantinople (Istanbul) (from AD 360), 2013
Drawing showing the layout and orientation of the Justinian-era marble floor slabs within the original interior at the time containing the ambo referred to by Paul the Silentiary.

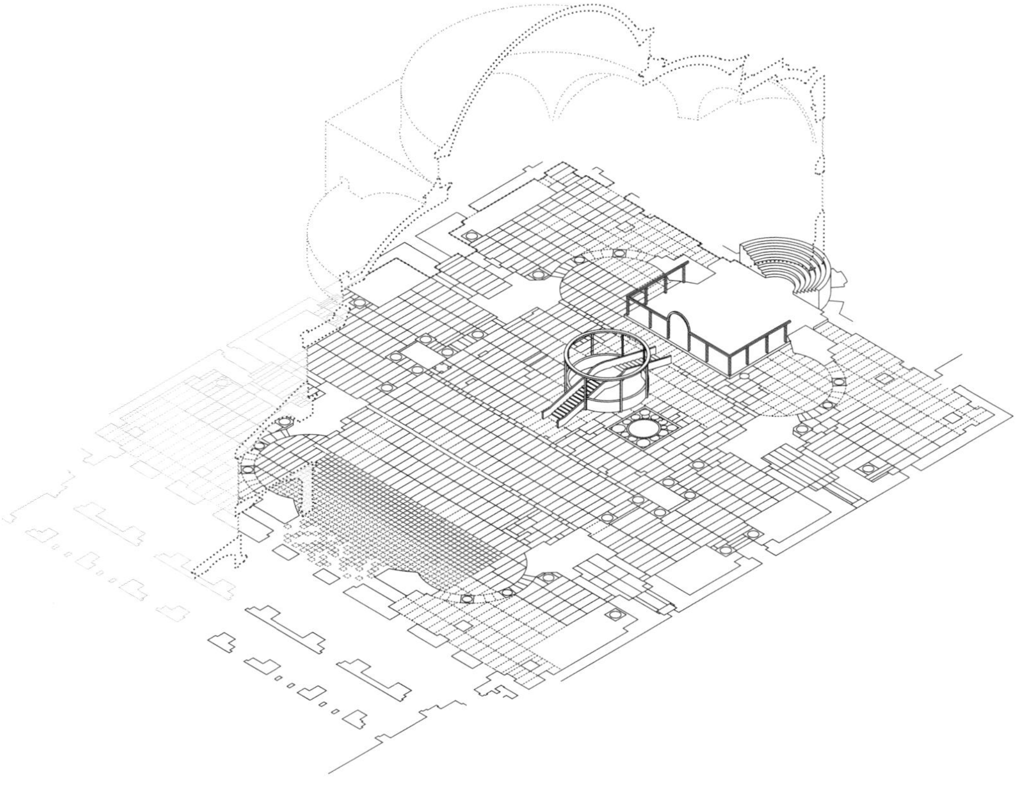

Detail of Proconnesian marble floor, Hagia Sophia, Constantinople (Istanbul), from AD 360
Paul the Silentiary's 6th-century description of the ambo – 'And as an island rises amidst the waves of the sea' – suggests the metaphor of the frozen sea evoked so clearly by the slabs of Proconnesian marble.

it takes its name from the full Greek title of the Hagia Sophia (Shrine of the Holy Wisdom of God). In all the original studies about this church, the composition of the church floors proved of particular interest. This can be traced back to Lethaby's influential summary of his thoughts on iconography in *Architecture, Mysticism and Myth* of 1891,[15] in which he devoted two chapters to floors: the first (Chapter VII), entitled 'The Labyrinth', looks at the labyrinth as a recurring symbol in pavement design; while the second, 'Pavements like the Sea' (Chapter XI), is a short but brilliant summary on the role that the floor has in sacred spaces across a wide range of cultures and periods, representing a cosmic realm. He pointed to an Assyrian pavement in the British Museum entirely patterned with lotus; to the black polished reflective stone in front of Pheidias' enthroned Zeus at the temple of Zeus at Olympia – 'A representation of the sea of heaven with its stars is especially appropriate to the floor of the holy place, which bears the figure of the god, or the altar'[16] – and speculated on the evidence that the Byzantine floors of the upper ambulatory at the Hagia Sophia were intended to symbolise a celestial sea. At the time of Lethaby's speculation, the building was used as a mosque and the main floor of the nave was covered in carpets. It was revealed for the first time since the 17th century in 1935 when under President Atatürk the building was turned into a museum. The massive slabs that make up the nave of the Hagia Sophia are Proconnesian marble, named after the island of Proconnesus (present-day Marmara Adasi in Turkey) from which it was extracted.

This coarse variegated marble was renowned in antiquity; large quantities were exported to Greece to carve into sarcophagi, and later it made up a great deal of the walling for the Byzantine city of Constantinople. Like many sources of stone in the same territory, it can vary hugely in character. This marble could provide a very even, clear, white type, but also came in a grey-veined form with a hint of green background that was chosen for the floor of the nearby Church of the Holy Apostles (*c* 536–550; now demolished) –

built, like the Hagia Sophia, by the Emperor Justinian I (*c* 482–565). In the Hagia Sophia, the staggering effect of the cascade of the dome with its ring of lantern windows, semi-domes and squinches, mediating between pierced walls to achieve the clear span of 30 metres (100 feet), has been movingly described at various points of the church's history.[17]

Justinian's expenditure on the Hagia Sophia was astounding. It was massive in scale and remained the world's largest cathedral for a thousand years. With its many chapels and shrines, gilded octagonal dome and mosaics, its interior was sumptuously decorated. It was purported that forty thousand pounds of silver went into the sanctuary alone.[18] Through its very splendour, the Hagia Sophia provided the Eastern Orthodox Church with a highly majestic presence in Constantinople. While the figurative mosaics were not introduced until after the period of iconoclasm in the 9th century, it is clear that the surfaces were intricately articulated, and the capitals and dosserets elaborately carved; a panoply of liturgical furniture, hangings and screens in precious metals and polychromatic stones were installed. The floor, though, is the exception, relying on its sheer expanse of book-matched, veined marble flagstones to speak to the faithful, and on its clear association with water. From antiquity to the European enlightenment and to this day in poetic interpretations, marble is understood as a metamorphosis of liquid into stone, its shimmering, polished qualities combining with its veining to suggest the movement of waves.

Thrust into the celestial sea floor of the Hagia Sophia is the circular ambo from which the priest would recite from

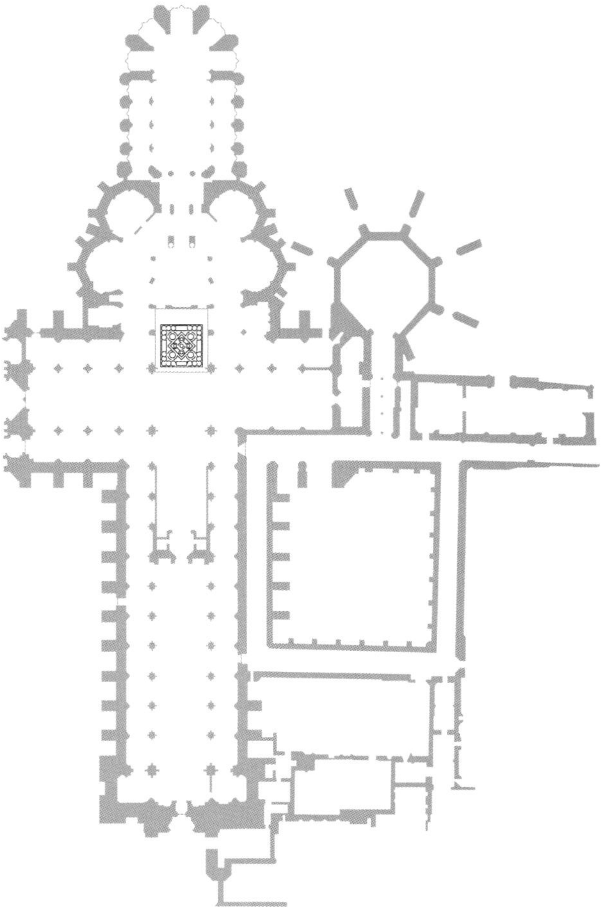

Eric Parry Architects, plan of Westminster Abbey, London (from AD 1090), 2013
The plan illustrates the location of the sanctuary and Edward the Confessor's Chapel, both subject to the Cosmati craftsmen's art.

biblical texts, emerging and retiring by means of a raised causeway connecting to the solea and the sanctuary of the altar. The imperial marshal Paul the Silentiary, commenting on the ambo of the Hagia Sophia in his famous eulogy to the cathedral after the reconstruction of the dome in 563, made the iconographic connection between the marble floor and the sea quite clear:

> And as an island rises amidst the waves of the sea … while the travellers are gladdened by it … so in the midst of the boundless temple rises upright the tower-like ambo of stone adorned with its meadow of marble, wrought with the beauty of the craftsman's art … it rather resembles some wave-lashed land … Projecting into the watery deep.[19]

The watery floor lying under the celestial sphere of a golden dome 'is a simulacrum of God's separation of the waters in Genesis 1:2–8': 'And the spirit of God moved upon the face of the water … and God made

Cosmati Pavement, Westminster Abbey, London, 1268
The Cosmati or Great Pavement of the sanctuary at Westminster Abbey, seen normally in anamorphic perspective by the human eye, centred on an onyx disk representing the unformed matter of a cosmic beginning.

the firmament, and divided the waters which were under the firmament from the waters which were above the firmament … And God called the firmament "heaven".'[20]

Turning westwards and northwards, unexpectedly perhaps to London, we find one of the greatest masterpieces of pavement crafting in the so-called Cosmati Pavement in the sanctuary of Westminster Abbey. Like the floor of the Hagia Sophia, this work has attracted intense interest, and an extensive bibliography of primary and secondary sources exists. I was first drawn to it as a rather mysterious presence because it was covered by carpet and was ceremoniously uncovered for a day in the year and for regal occasions like coronations; thankfully it has recently undergone an exercise in conservation, and since 2010 has been permanently on view to public scrutiny.[21] The pavement has been attributed with medieval mystical significance throughout its history. According to a 15th-century monk at Westminster Abbey, Richard

Eric Parry Architects, drawing of the Cosmati Pavement at Westminster Abbey, London (1268), 2013
The drawing incorporates Richard Foster's interpretation of the original Latin inscription set in brass letters as well as of the intended meaning, from Foster's 'Symbolic schema of the pavement's central quincunx', published in his *Patterns of Thought* (1991).

Sporley, the pavement and its inscription symbolised the world, or the universe, and its end.[22] In 1991, a book devoted to the history and meaning of the pavement was published entitled *Patterns of Thought: The Hidden Meaning of the Great Pavement of Westminster Abbey*, by Richard Foster.[23] The work has been identified reasonably conclusively to Italian craftsmen belonging to a group known as the Cosmati. The families involved with this signature form of ornament, used both for architectural artefacts like ciboria, tombs and candelabra, as well as for pavements, were active for about two centuries. Their work involved the cutting of stone 'opus sectile', as opposed to the mosaicist's craft of placing small units of the same size, usually square. The materials the Cosmati used were a mix of marbles, limestones and granites, often local, with their trademark green and purple porphyries and other rare stones reused from ruins of classical buildings, and notably during this period unavailable because the source quarries had been lost to contemporary medieval use.

The Mnemonic Device

The immense mnemonic capacity of a pavement is vividly illustrated by two final examples: the ongoing Europe-wide Stolpersteine project by artist Gunter Demnig, and the plan formed by pilgrims' repeated passage around the sacred water basin of Banganga Tank in India.

The latter is situated at the centre of the village of Walkeshwar, one of the seven islands joined over the last two centuries to form the metropolis of Mumbai. The site has been a point of pilgrimage for about a thousand years and its legendary origin is based on an episode in the epic tale of Rama Dasarathi, the seventh reincarnation of the god Vishnu. A stepped water basin hewn out of the basalt rock is a composite derived from *bana* (arrow) and *ganga* (sacred stream). When Rama arrived at Walkeshwar he was thirsty from his travels, so he took an arrow and shot it into the ground. Water sprang forth and he drank; the spring he created is the course of Banganga Tank rising on the northeast corner. It is thus a *tirtha* (place of pilgrimage), and once the religious significance is understood the formal topography becomes clear.

The approach to Banganga is by a street known as Ladder Street, and at the top of the hill above the village the circumambulation of the sacred waters of the tank begins, proceeding in a clockwise direction. It is immediately clear

Banganga Tank (first built 12th century, reconstruction 18th century) and Walkeshwar village, Mumbai, India: site plan
At the centre is the rock-cut stepped water basin, and surrounding it a dense grouping of temples and sacred landscapes of many different scales that are ranged along the circumambulatory path of pilgrims.

from the plan that all the buildings – mainly hostels, temples and a multitude of shrines – relate to this rite of passage. The route is intended to reveal and incorporate all the aspects of the divine and represents the lifelong journey and all the various qualities of manifest divinity, by participating in which the pilgrim can obtain *moksa* – final release. Walkeshwar is built and understood as the *imago mundi* – a microcosm. At the centre of the tank and the circumambulation rises a wooden pole located on a stone base which is the *axis mundi* of this microcosm, with the tank representing the cosmic ocean. The pole symbolises the great rod fixed to Vishnu the turtle's back, which the gods struggled over and so churned the ocean to create the ordered world. The slopes are negotiated by street-wide cut steps. The surface is made of accumulated dust like a makeup over the natural stone bed, all living material – an animated world of libations and purificatory rites.

The other example is the Stolpersteine (literally meaning 'stumbling stones') project conceived by the Cologne-born artist Gunter Demnig. Begun in 1995, it consists of non-ferrous alloy cubes with 94-millimetre (3¾-inch) sides (to fit a 100-millimetre (3⅞-inch) grid), each stamped with a first and family name, date of birth and date of deportation and standing in front of the building in which the particular Holocaust victim lived.

It is harrowing when the glint that appears at first sight as merely decorative becomes understood as a physical manifestation of such a tyrannical clinical atrocity. The extraordinary project is extending like a cleansing stain across Europe, most recently in Rome. Nowhere in my urban wanderings has the feeling of nausea been more marked than in a side alley named Martin-Luther-King-Platz in Hamburg – now a patch of pavement between an underground car park entrance and a service yard off the fast-paced Grindelallee in Hamburg's Eimsbüttel district, on the edge of a leafy university quarter – where, almost like a gaming board, 31 of these 'stumbling' blocks are placed with one that states:

Hier stand ein
jüdisches
WAISENHAUS
BIS 1942
[Here stood a Jewish orphanage until 1942]

Gunter Demnig, Stolpersteine, Martin-Luther-King-Platz, Hamburg, Germany, 1995
A harrowing example of the Stolpersteine ('stumbling stones') project by artist Gunter Demnig, started in 1995 in Cologne, now present throughout Germany and being picked up in other European countries. Each named cube, with sides measuring 94 millimetres (3¾-inches), represents an individual deportation to the Nazi extermination camps.

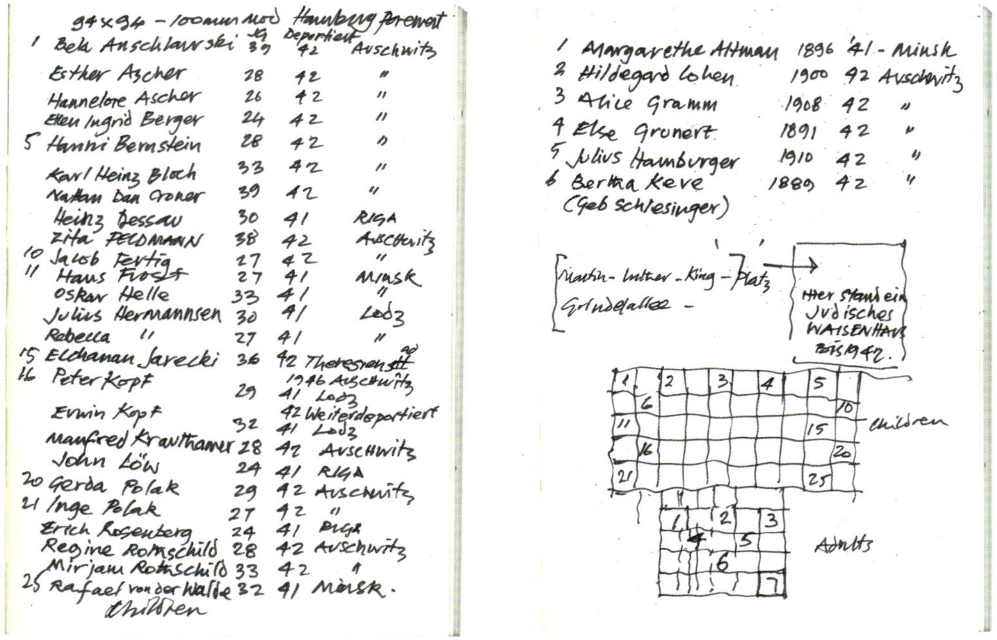

Twenty-five children between the ages of three and eighteen and six adults between the ages of 32 and 51, deported in 1941 and 1942 to certain death, before the harrowing bombing of the city that eradicated so many buildings in July 1943.

Eric Parry, personal annotations, Hamburg, Germany, April 2012
A list of the Holocaust victims from the Jewish Orphanage in Martin-Luther-King-Platz, from my notebook.

With so many other tantalising examples unexplored because of limited space, at least between the Boyle Family and the Waisenhaus the significance of the palimpsest of urban life understood through the pavement stands as a reminder against the tide of asphalt neutrality. The necessarily planimetric focus of this chapter on the surfaces of the ground has nonetheless hints of the perspectival results: the reflectivity of Lisbon's streets; the anamorphic character of a Cosmati pavement; the mesmeric reflection of Proconnesian marble slabs in the Hagia Sophia. Now, raising our gaze leads naturally to the next chapter: 'Horizon'.

References

1. See Guy Debord, *The Society of the Spectacle* [*La Société du spectacle*, 1967], translated by Donald Nicholson-Smith, Zone Books (New York), 1995.
2. Charles Dickens, *Our Mutual Friend* [1864–5], Modern Library (New York), 2002, passim.
3. TS Eliot, *The Waste Land* [1922], in *Selected Poems*, Faber and Faber (London), 1969, p 53: lines 60–63.
4. Álvaro Siza in conversation with the author, Porto, September 2011.
5. Álvaro Siza, personal letter to the author, 25 February 2013.
6. Voltaire, *Candide or Optimism* [*Candide, ou l'Optimisme*, 1759], translated by Peter Constantine, Modern Library (New York), 2005, p 16.
7. The term *jaula* employed by Siza means 'animal cage', as opposed to the original phrase *gaiola pombalina*, where *gaiola* means 'bird cage'. The phrase *gaiola pombalina* has traditionally been used to describe this structure, in possible reference to the original 18th-century scale models. Ironically, *pombal* means 'dovecote', from which follows that *gaiola pombalina* would mean literally 'Pombal's bird cage'.
8. Jorge Sampaio, President of Portugal, 'Speech at the Netherlands Architecture Institute' (Rotterdam, 1997), quoted in Álvaro Siza, Dominique Machabert, Emílio de Santiago *et al*, *The Reconstruction of the Chiado: Lisbon*, ICEP (Porto), 1997, p 9.
9. Siza, Machabert, De Santiago *et al* 1997, p 120.
10. Richard Edlund and Örjan Molander, *Stortorget, från brunn till P-mätare*, Kalmar Läns Museum (Kalmar), 1998.
11. In Helena Mattsson (ed), *Kalmar Stortorg: Art/Architecture in Urban Space*, The National Public Art Council Sweden, 2005, p 132.
12. *Ibid* p 155.
13. *Ibid.*
14. William Lethaby, *Architecture, Mysticism and Myth*, Percival (London), 1891 and *The Church of Sancta Sophia, Constantinople: A Study of Byzantine Building*, Macmillan & Co (London), 1894.
15. Lethaby 1891.
16. *Ibid* p 214.
17. For an excellent interpretative and searching essay see Fabio Barry, 'Walking on Water: Cosmic Floors in Antiquity and the Middle Ages', *The Art Bulletin*, vol 89, no 4, December 2007, pp 627–56: http://www.jstor.org/discover/10.2307/25067354?uid=43145&uid=3738032&uid=2129&uid=68&uid=2&uid=70&uid=3&uid=43144&uid=62&sid=21101867176127 (accessed 19 November 2014).
18. *Ibid* p 627.
19. *Ibid* p 647.
20. *Ibid* p 634.
21. For further information on the conservation of the pavement see: http://www.westminster-abbey.org/conservation (accessed 19 November 2014).
22. *Ibid.*
23. Richard Foster, *Patterns of Thought: The Hidden Meaning of the Great Pavement of Westminster Abbey*, Jonathan Cape (London), 1991.

2 Horizon

The horizon poses a fascinating philosophical conundrum; it cannot be removed and yet it cannot be reached, and in this state of permanence and ambiguity it creates the space for advancing literally and figuratively. An accessible horizon would de facto destroy the space within which the body exists and indeed the means by which it can be represented. *Horizon* has etymological roots in the Greek ὁρίζω, 'to delimit', and a horizon marks the boundary of the visual field at the meeting of the terrestrial and celestial, while also metaphorically underpinning the idea of discovery and the setting of new objectives ('new horizons'). The horizon cuts across the spatial distinction between inside and outside. In the horizon, exteriority merges with interiority.

'The horizon is the translation of man into the world … man lives in the horizon, the horizon is himself, the horizon is the world, the horizon reflects back to him the human world, namely the world as visible in the beam of human reflection.'[1] Thus the philosopher Cornelius A van Peursen has summed up the critical relationship between dwelling and situation, and their interdependence with horizon. In the same essay he also illustrated how horizon cuts across the inside–outside distinction, belonging to us while remaining beyond us. Horizon, unlike an object in a landscape or still-life painting that can be moved or distributed but is always situated relative to ourselves, remains inaccessible, mysterious and in the realm of reverie. On a cusp between Impressionism and Cubism, Paul Cézanne's (1839–1906) late works oscillate between the horizon of the table in his still lifes (and in particular those of skulls, of which the art critic Joachim Gasquet related that Cézanne 'in his last mornings, clarified the idea that death is a heaping together of bony boxes where the eye sockets give off a bluish thought'[2]) and the horizon of the landscape punctuated by his Mont Sainte-Victoire 'motif' which he painted repeatedly.

These paintings eloquently illustrate Van Peursen's summary of the qualities of horizon and the continuum of exterior and interior. There is a more literal continuity in the vexed question of the placing of objects in relation to the horizon, a violation of the natural order that defines context on a horizon – from those of prehistory to the very contemporary debate of the metamorphosis of London's skyline. In the landscapes of Neolithic settlement the specific placement of upright stones relative to horizon is a crucial part of the setting for ritual and belief, evidenced by the lines and clusters of stones from northern Scotland to the Palaggiu of Corsica in the Mediterranean. We remain justifiably awestruck by the feats of these constructions, the shaping

Callanish Stones, Calanais, Isle of Lewis, Scotland, 3000 BC
At the centre of a circle of stones is a monolith 5 metres (16 feet) high and 1.5 metres (5 feet) in breadth. The powerful configuration, shown here at dawn, lies on a ridge above a long finger of sea-loch water and a backdrop of Hebridean hills.

of igneous rock, the movement of stones over prodigious distances such as those that the builders of Stonehenge undertook from the Pembrokeshire coast to Salisbury Plain and then the placement of those massive lintel blocks that themselves represent a horizon created by artifice. The artificial lowering of the horizon by building a vantage point from which to be the first to see and thus literally to rule over, has been an act of empowerment understood by the heaping up of material. From earthen banks this was drawn early in the Bronze Age to an extraordinary sophistication in the battered dovetailed masonry of the megalithic defensive keeps exemplified by the quatrefoil 20-metre- (65-foot-) high walls of Su Nuraxi in Sardinia. Ritual domination is exemplified by the mud-brick ziggurats of the Elamites and of course the Pyramids of Egypt.

Horizon and Language

A town with an encircling wall could have been construed as a haven against marauding aggression or a girdle of oppression. Psychologically, the topography one grows up with is deeply embedded in the homeland, *die Heimat*. Frequently, the shock of the 'new' aside, those who move within an undulating hilly landscape feel to different degrees an agoraphobic anxiety when confronted with flat coastal or prairie landscapes, and vice versa.

The relative quantum of sky that one is used to is part of a deep-rooted sense of spatial ease or comfort – and the cultural manifestation is shockingly stark and obvious. A landlocked and mountainous country like Switzerland is bordered by three languages: French to the west, German, the dominant language, to the north and east, and Italian to the south. Over time all three have met their topographical boundary through the sheer impenetrability of rock and forest. There is in origin a fourth Swiss language, Romansh, spoken now by less than 35,000: in the entirely mountainous Canton of Graubünden, Romansh is an umbrella for a group of closely related dialects – at least for those officially recognised and only standardised in 1982. The main ones are Sursilvan, Sutsilvan, Surmiran, Putèr, Vallader, Jauer and Rumantsch Grischun. Joseph von Planta, who became the Principal Librarian of the British Museum from 1799–1827, was of Romansh-Swiss origin and in 1775 wrote an account of the Romansh language that was published the following year.[3]

The little connection here is in mountainous countries between the inhabitants of the different valleys and the absolute independence of each jurisdiction, which further lessens the frequency of their intercourse – and also accounts, in a great measure, for the variety of secondary dialects subsisting in almost every different community or even village.[4]

This is in contrast to the vast stain of the common language of the Anglo-Saxons, which spread from the Baltic and the Angeln peninsula through to the English Midlands, northwards to Scotland and southwards: the Low German language known as *Plattdüütsch* or *Nedderdüütsch*, where 'low' refers to the plains and coastal areas of northern Europe between the North Sea and Baltic Sea. Alongside the commonality of language comes trade, and during the relatively stable Early Middle Ages new settlements emerged responsively. The common roots of urban form with local topographic inflections and cultural assimilations are immediately as striking as the linguistic parallels. The magnum opus of the important urban topographer Mario Morini,[5] whose focus within his wide-ranging study published in 1963 remains the Italian city and its roots in Roman and pre-Roman settlement, draws out an underlying common spatial and cultural ground. The same is true of the cities of the Baltic Sea, and particularly those associated with the Hanseatic League of merchant guilds, mostly founded in the 12th and 13th centuries but rarely studied recently because of the political divisions of the second half of the 20th century (and almost entirely absent from Morini's work). The Hanseatics had their historical centre around Lübeck, spreading eastwards along the southern shores of the Baltic from Kiel to Wismar, Rostock, Stralsund and Greifswald. Beyond the current national boundaries they included the Teutonic cities of Memel (now Klaipéda, Lithuania), Königsberg (now Kaliningrad, Russia), Elbing (now Elbląg, Poland), Danzig (now Gdańsk, Poland), Culm (now Chełmno, Poland) and Toruń (Poland). Westwards from Lübeck their web included Hamburg, Bremen and the important inland city of Lüneburg, the centre for salt production in northern Europe with an output of 20,000 tons from fifty saltworks in 1276. With many of their trading hosts they built storage, dockside and administrative centres like the Tyskebryggen in Bergen (Norway), the Oosters Huis in Antwerp (Belgium), the Peterhof in Novgorod (Russia) and the Stalhof in London. They ultimately formed a mercantile web identifiable not through the dominant buildings of an overlord but by a unique balance of urban communities, likened by some scholars to the repetitive organisation of a Cistercian monastery.[6] They were ruled by a secular council, the Rat, made up of between 12 and 30 members who were appointed for life while looking after their own businesses; and from among the Rat's members were periodically chosen pairs of burgomasters, a balance evocatively depicted

Caspar David Friedrich, *Greifswald im Mondschein* (*Griefswald by Moonlight*), oil on canvas, 1817
Caspar David Friedrich paints the silhouette of his Hanseatic hometown collaged into a fictional and sombre foreground framing the perspective of the central spire at nightfall.

in Thomas Mann's 1901 novel *Buddenbrooks*. This structure ensured the avoidance of singular autocratic rule and, through the trades, a more complex ordering instantly distinguishable in the multiplicity of sacred buildings in each city. The latter form further connects with other cities, as is the case with the churches of St Jakobi (St James) which together form the northerly projection of the *Jakobsweg* leading through France and on to the pilgrimage destination of Santiago de Compostela in northern Spain. Most of the cities contain a church dedicated to the cult of the Virgin Mary, and likewise to St Nicholas and often the Holy Ghost.

The Collective Skyline

The reason for dwelling, albeit very briefly, on the structure of the Hanseatic cities is that their political, trading and sacred structures created a very recognisable skyline of multiple towers and spires, and thus the preoccupation with city silhouette was deeply embedded in the northern psyche.

As an example of this, one can begin to look to the representation of these cities in painting, and nowhere more strikingly than in the works of Caspar David Friedrich (1774–1840). He is paradoxically best known for his *The Wanderer above the Sea of Fog* (1818; Kunsthalle, Hamburg) – a Nietzschean depiction of an urbane figure dressed in dark green velvet suit, cane in hand, back to the observer, astride a mountain crag overlooking an Alpine landscape with the horizon, below, obscured by mist and cloud. The landscapes of his early life were however the northern lowlands of the Baltic, around Griefswald where he was born. He sketched prolifically, taking these studies back to his studio where he assembled the elements of his observation into the Romantic paintings for which he is justly honoured. Some good examples are several paintings that involve the Griefswald skyline set in the fore- and middle grounds by his imagination. In one it is heathland with horses, an Arcadian vision of a heavenly city viewed at daybreak, a pastel dream; in another it is the gloom of the *Abenddämmerung* (dusk), sticky with the sweat of human toil. In each, the position of church towers remains a static memorable composition.

Each city would have been experienced however as a slowly moving kinetic composition of very legible elements, understood as a whole. In contrast to the rapidity of approach mentioned earlier in this chapter, these cities emerged from the horizon, by sea or land, accompanied by the cycle of day and night. Instead of a stopwatch, one needs to think in terms of the duration of a pilgrimage, of a reading of Chaucer's *Canterbury Tales*, or of the figures awaiting the return of a masted sailing boat slowly emerging from the horizon of the sea – very much the equivalent of its city's towers.

Eric Parry, sketch map of the main Hanseatic cities, 2014
Circles indicate the main cities of the Hanseatic League along the north Baltic coast.

Eric Parry, sketch plan of the historic centre of Stralsund, 2014
The colour coding indicates the principal buildings: the Rathaus (brown); the Church of St Nicholas (blue); the Church of St Mary (red); the Church of St James (verdigris); and Holy Ghost hospice and convent of St Catherine (green).

While the cities of the Hanseatic League have suffered cycles of destruction, and never more so than in the 20th century, they have survived rebuilding and economic eclipse remarkably well. Stralsund, after Lübeck the most important Hanseatic town on the Baltic, is an excellent example of the disposition of parts. Girdled by a typically strong defensive wall, it faces eastwards to the Baltic Sea, protected by the land of the island of Rügen, and westwards towards the cities of Rostock and Lübeck. Within the walls, the most important civic space is the market square. This is formed on three sides by burgher houses with their combination of familial, business and storage spaces. On its south side is the Rathaus – essentially a three-storey structure of cellars, open arcaded market at ground level and the ceremonial Rat meeting spaces on the first floor. Immediately in front of this is the Church of St Nicholas with its mighty two-towered west facade. To lend the Rathaus more presence on the square, the six-gabled elevation is raised as a screen to the height of the aisle walls of the church, a complex lattice of brickwork that casts its delicate frame in shadow on the pavement. St Nicholas's was the church of the Rat and held their pantheon, evident in the altars, stalls and monuments. With its two towers, it was the most significant mass on the skyline. At a respectful, or competitive, distance, the cloth workers built a particularly fine church, the Church of St Mary, with a most imposing single tower and whose ambition for height is evident in the massive piers around which the delicate envelope of the church expands. To the south and east of the marketplace is the third great church of the town, St James, funded by another set of guilds. To these four great civic structures are added the Dominican convent of St Catherine and the hospice of the Holy Ghost. The landward approaches are now diminished by the inevitable growth of modern suburbs, but from the sea it is still a striking composition of towers breaking the horizon. Moving from open water, they become visible and then legible relative to each other, slowly twisting in changing masses and spacings but soon discernible as the particular configuration of Stralsund. Each of these Baltic ports carries the common traces of the several and the whole, the complex patterns of Brick Gothic and the art of silhouette. While the repetitions are confusing to the outsider, their differences are immediate to their own community. Like the silhouette of a face which is a

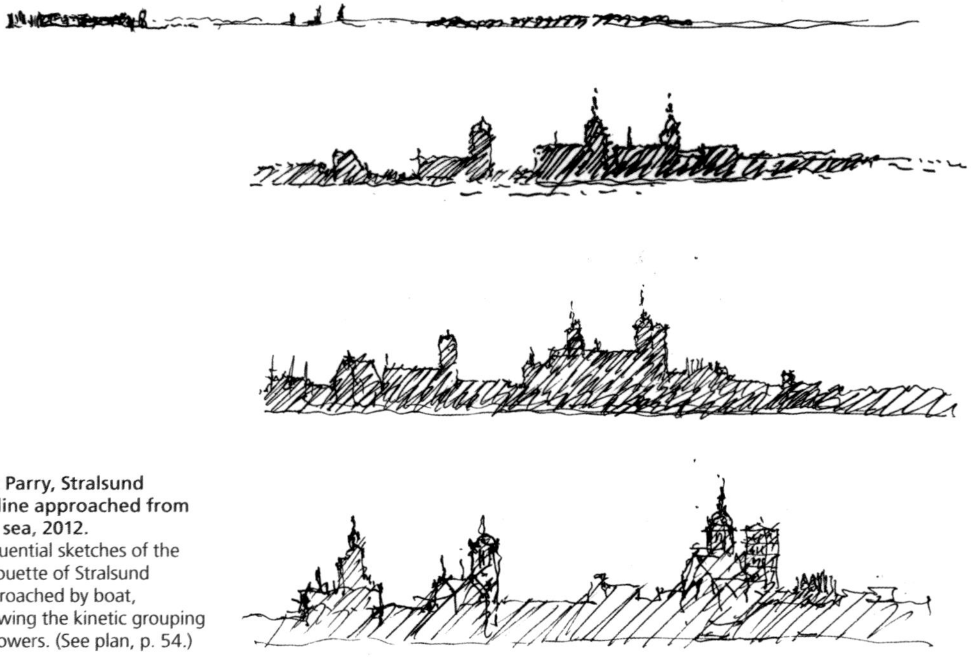

Eric Parry, Stralsund skyline approached from the sea, 2012.
Sequential sketches of the silhouette of Stralsund approached by boat, showing the kinetic grouping of towers. (See plan, p. 54.)

compression of complexity, texture and depth into an identifiable profile, cities are summarised through their skyline, the diagrammatisation of their monumental buildings in coins, treatises and topographical representations.

The Rise of London's Skyline

The speed and focused destinations of transport systems that deliver from one global point to another by air, rail and road, with the least impediments and stoppages possible, deny us the slow anticipation of approach that was a part of pre-industrial travel. It is a well-trodden discourse. Cities are revealed from the aerial holding patterns that result from overstretched civil aviation systems or the pace of expansion joints on aerial motorways, in a linear perspective articulately described in books like Deyan Sudjic's *The 100 Mile City* (1992). The child assumes from these perspectives that the panorama is the equivalent to the setting in a playroom: miniaturised, and denied mass and proportion beyond the two-dimensionality of a mapped projection. The metaphor of the playroom is extended and lived out at the annual global property fairs, and nowhere more prominently than at MIPIM (Marché international des professionnels de l'immobilier), held in the pre-season spring of Cannes on France's Mediterranean coast. Here cities arrive in model form accompanied by mayors, politicians and planners. Notable are those of Paris's La Défense, the City of London, Frankfurt, but also a myriad of satellite cities. Their partners in this choreography of cities are the developers, fund managers and contractors. Like a control room in a James Bond movie, buildings light up and are transposed and enlarged as the future of city form is played out in a game of supply, demand, opportunity and a sprinkling of constraints, the latter generally packed away for the later stages of the game.

In London today, we are living through one of these seismic shifts in the metamorphosis of city skylines: compare Visscher's 1616 view of the city (illustrated in Chapter 1) with Canaletto's view of c 1746–50, painted after the reconstruction that followed the 1666 Great Fire of London, in which a flurry of church steeples form a backdrop to Sir Christopher Wren's (1632–1723) St Paul's Cathedral, sweeping away to Wren's monument to that fire and London Bridge. A similar view from

Anonymous, 'Oilcan City', *New York Evening Journal*, undated
Following the exhibition of the first public proposals for what would develop as the Rockefeller Center in March 1931, the *New York Evening Journal* published a cartoon lampooning the development as 'Oilcan City'. Almost prophetically, the 'Oilcan City' cartoon anticipated today's standard nicknaming of buildings as household objects.

Giovanni Antonio Canal (Canaletto), *The Thames from Somerset House Terrace towards the City*, c 1746–50
A view of the London landscape and some of its most traditional references well before the concept of skyline came to the fore: river, banks, town, and St Paul's Cathedral as a beacon on the horizon.

the 1930s incorporating the Victorian embankment is much denser on the ground, but the skyline remains remarkably intact two centuries later. After the massive destruction of the Second World War, the tentative rising of the city skyline took shape in the residential towers of the Barbican Estate, first proposed as part of the ambitious masterplan in 1959 but not realised until the 1970s, and the NatWest Tower (1981), designed by Richard Seifert.

In the wake of the property boom that accompanied the 'Big Bang' deregulation of City financial markets in 1987, the City of London – with its constrained medieval street pattern and long-established quarters for insurance and banking, together with the tapestry of livery company landownership – has been galvanised into an unprecedented sprint of development, goaded by competition from the European banking industry focused on the German city of Frankfurt and by the relatively free hand of the London Docklands Development Corporation at Canary Wharf. Because of protected viewing corridors, a new planning and development strategy was devised for the City that would be permissive and encouraging to developers but rather autocratic in its choice of architects. In creating the cluster of tall buildings, the City aldermen courted the displeasure of other London Boroughs, English Heritage and, more generally, conservative forces led by the Prince of Wales and international bodies such as UNESCO.

Henry Turner, *Lighters moored in the King's Reach*, 1935/1936
A photograph of the eastward view from Waterloo Bridge.

In the enabling of development, the City planning authority led by Peter Rees, Chief Planning Officer from 1988 to 2014, was pivotal in brokering marriages between the herd of predatory developers with a focus on the bottom line and architects considered to have the ambition and skill to create innovation and, in league with marketing agents, the necessary stand-out qualities of the one-liner. So it is that, between 2001 and 2003, the building by Foster + Partners quickly dubbed 'The Gherkin' appeared, to house the insurance company Swiss Re. The force of its form, with a double-layered skin of glass encapsulating the heavily clad basketweave structure, rises surreally like a space rocket from a 1950s Dan Dare comic book – unfortunately incapable of lifting off to leave a decently proportioned city square. Separated by a decade and an intervening financial slump is Rogers Stirk Harbour + Partners' Leadenhall Building (2014), better known as the 'Cheesegrater': a deft blow across the block conveniently created the tapered profile to allow views of St Paul's Cathedral from Fleet Street to be unencumbered. It is not the only building to have been designed to skulk behind others on the horizon when

Eric Parry, City of London skyline, 2006
Sketch illustrating the proposed buildings, most of which have been built. Their nomenclature and character have an uncanny echo in the cartoon on page 56.

viewed from prescribed locations. Moor House (2005), another Foster + Partners design, actually takes the form of the shadow of the cathedral's dome as viewed from London Wall. These forms, while arresting, create the need for structural gymnastics – in the case of the Cheesegrater, a considerable additional tonnage of steel to allow for the phenomenal torsional stresses created in the asymmetry and celebrated aesthetically in the massive north wall incorporating in it Rogers's cannon, the manifestation of circulation through the exposed lifts that animate this otherwise blank 206-metre- (676-foot-) high city wall.

Horizon as City Spectacle

A sketch I produced in 2006 of the emerging City of London skyline was drawn up before most of the significant recent buildings were executed. The City 'cluster' was enthusiastically embraced by the planners and the business community alike, and was endorsed by the then Mayor of London, Ken Livingstone. It was to be a landscape with a 'peak' and lower 'foothills'.

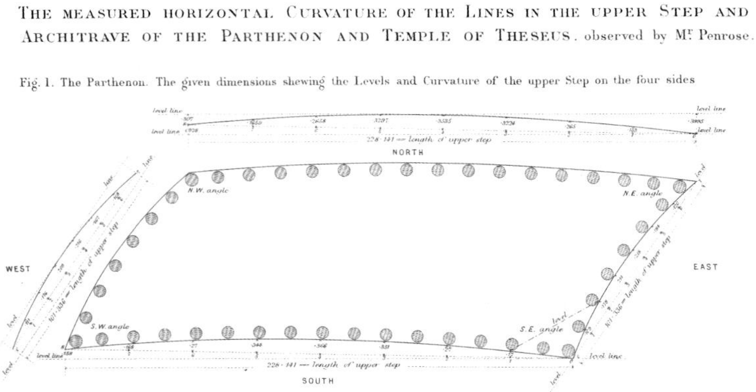

'The Measured Horizontal Curvature of the Lines in the Upper Step and Architrave of the Parthenon and Temple of Theseus, observed by Mr Penrose', in John Pennethorne, *The Geometry and Optics of Ancient Architecture*, 1878 (part III, pl III)
Analysis of the convexity of the stylobate of the Parthenon observed by Mr Penrose and drawn by John Pennethorne, as published in his monumental treatise of 1878.

Edwin Lutyens, detail of the Cenotaph, Whitehall, London, 1920
Dimensioned drawing, from Arthur Stanley George Butler, George Stewart and Christopher Hussey's *The Architecture of Sir Edwin Lutyens* (Country Life and Charles Scribner's Sons, London and New York, 1950, vol III, pl LXV). Note the subtlety of the imperial increments but also the terrestrial radius of 900 feet (274 metres) and celestial of approximately 1000 feet (300 metres).

The sketch was both a topographical description of the unbuilt – the Heron, the Cheesegrater, the Helter-Skelter and the Walkie-Talkie – but also of the deathly bottle-green glass of the cladding of most contemporary commercial buildings. In the gap between the Walkie-Talkie (2014, by Rafael Viñoly; more formally known as 20 Fenchurch Street) and the cluster was the simple white tower of my 2006 proposal for Generali – since redesigned as a lower city block with a public roof garden now under construction. Viñoly's warped tower, larger in plan the further it extended upwards – to obvious bottom-line applause – is an anomaly and illustrative of the system of planning in the City of the time. Even shortened as it was in the process of dialogue between the consenting parties to its design, it could not be supported as a part of the cluster or indeed the foothills. In the desire to add to the list of world-class architects that parallel their instantly nicknameable formal compositions, the City was prepared to make an exception to the rule. The reasoning that was put forward at one meeting was that the Viñoly proposal was exceptional, a talisman – like the 'prow of a ship'; and so it stands now in its lumpen droop beyond the cluster, bowing immodestly to Renzo Piano's Shard (2013) to the south of the river. The canting low-iron glass walls of the Shard, built close to the site of the struggle between the City and Southwark (see Chapter 1), caused consternation in the City. However, it presaged another chapter in London's tall buildings beyond the dialogue between Canary Wharf and the City of London. It was, as is now evident, only the prologue to an orgy of tall buildings over 20 storeys – some three hundred and fifty currently in the making – that will transform and arguably overwhelm London from a particular skyline broken by the white stone filigree of buildings signifying community to one of green glass envelopes imported from far afield, representing the Faustian pact of national commerce and real estate.

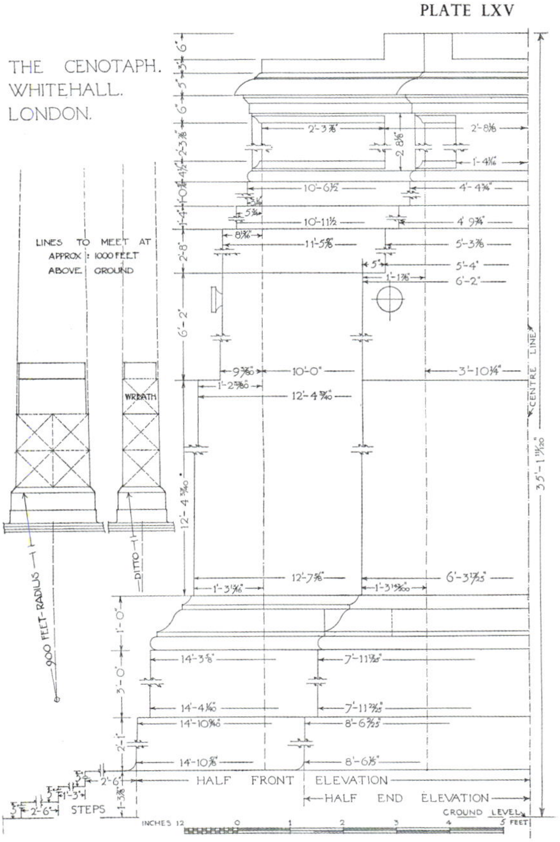

The Wellbeing of Horizon

An uninterrupted horizon between, for instance, the sea and the sky always tends towards the convex, both literally and psychologically. To see the line drawn down implies the terror of a whirlpool, to be drawn into the depths. The curvature of the earth is an unseen presence as fundamental as orientation. A leaning tower threatens collapse as the hunching of a body does in old age and as a sagging structure suggests ruin. Subtle optical adjustments, that the eye may not immediately register but that the mind in a subliminal way does, have been a part of architectural practice for millennia, and nowhere more explicitly than Athens in the age of Pericles (c 495–429 BC). The whole lexicon of ancient Greek architecture, from the spacing of columns to the entasis and the orders, consists of essays in optical calibration. The 19th-century rediscovery of the sophistication of the relationship of the parts to the whole caused widespread awe, although these calibrations had been described by Vitruvius six centuries after their deployment.

Francis Cranmer Penrose (1817–1903), who became the first Director of the British School at Athens when it opened in 1865, had undertaken a remarkable measured survey of the Parthenon in 1846 following the first observations about a decade before. This was a task easier said than done, as it required specialist surveying equipment being shipped to Athens and then the erection of scaffolding under the capitals of one section of the ruined building. What he was able to confirm was that all the horizontal lines of the Parthenon were in fact delicately convexly curved. John Pennethorne

(1808–1888) – the son of a key collaborator of the architect John Nash, who had undertaken detailed surveys of the elements of the building himself – published his magnum opus in 1878, from which illustration is taken. It states Penrose's precise measurements, a rise of 0.214 feet (65.2 millimetres) on the front and 0.354 feet (107.9 millimetres) on the flanks. The precision of the measurements is startling, being not just in tenths and hundredths but also thousandths of a foot.

What follows the slight curvature of the stylobate is the adjustment of the column bases, then exponentially the incline of the shafts and the resolution of the abacus with the pediment. When these adjustments are taken into consideration one is left, as Le Corbusier was in the section of *Towards a New Architecture* (1923) dedicated to the Parthenon,[7] marvelling at the skill of the Greek masons and architects in their combined efforts to satisfy the eye of the beholder, be they those of gods or humankind.

Towards the end of his career, Edwin Lutyens (1869–1944) was called to the task of designing monuments to the fallen of the First World War. The results include the cathedral-scale shell of Thiepval (1932) and the more modest-sized Cenotaph in Whitehall, London (1920). Why, one might ask, does this simple erect rectangle of Portland stone carry such authority? Undoubtedly it is the significance of what it represents and the undemonstrative emptiness of its surfaces, too small to hold a roll call of names. Fundamentally the answer lies in the technical illustration. As with the example of the Parthenon, it is calibrated to the thousandth of an inch, but additionally there are two remarkable notes: the first that stipulates a vanishing point 900 feet (274 metres) below the ground to which the plinth responds in curvature, like the hilt of a buried blade; and the second a celestial meeting point at a height of approximately 1,000 feet (300 metres), to which the faces of the rectangle step.

Moving forward in time to an example of horizon concerns in my own practice, 5 Aldermanbury Square (Eric Parry Architects, 2007) rests on ground once occupied by buildings adjacent to the crossing of the *cardo* (main road running north to south) and *decumanus* (main road running east to west) of the Roman fort which lay to the northwest of the town of Londinium. Given that the new building was to replace Richard Seifert's Royex House of 1962, which was still standing when the project began, it took some imagination first to roll back the waves of development between the two eras and then to begin to divine a possible future.

Eric Parry Architects, Aldermanbury Square, London, 2007: above-ground view showing the entasis of the facade
Southern elevation of 5 Aldermanbury Square showing the west and east wings, the outer elevations of which are offset from the vertical, from the 9th to the 18th floors, to a radius of 350 metres (1,150 feet).

Usefully, the area had been featured in an early sequence in the 1966 cult film *Blow-Up*, directed by Michelangelo Antonioni, a central force in post-war Italian cinematography whose work captures the complexities of the Italian modernist spirit. He had chosen the then recently completed ensemble of buildings along the new City Road, between Moorgate and Aldersgate, for a scene in which David Hemmings, in the central role of a restless fashion photographer, drives a convertible Rolls-Royce westwards between the enfilade of new near-identical curtain-walled office buildings 60 metres (200 feet) long, 16 metres (52 feet) wide and 53 metres (174 feet) high, set at an angle of 22 degrees to the road and picking up the orientation of the underlying Roman town. He swerves left, speaking into a Dictaphone, off the short dual carriageway to pass the Brewers Hall, a livery company headquarters newly built as well but looking like an emaciated classically dressed civic building, and then the entrance to Royex House. The sequence is fascinating for the surrounding wasteland, the remnants of a pre-existing Victorian order and the absence of urban clutter. It is framed between a scene of post-party revellers on the Economist Plaza in St James's and a fashion shoot in a Soho loft. This was Antonioni's London edit, but

roll on four decades and the perspective was quite changed. Antonioni's view has been blocked by a recent building straddling the road. Wood Street to the south of this had been transformed on its west side by a series of buildings adhering to a street cornice height set by the planners, resulting in good buildings, particularly number 88 (1999) by the Richard Rogers Partnership. To the east, the central section circles around the City Police Station building with its stables, cells and vehicle entrances forming the curtilage to the storeyed central tower. Designed by McMorran & Whitby in 1966, it is a particularly finely detailed Portland stone group and the rectangular tower deserves careful study not least for its subtle stepping. In plan the building frontage sets back to allow the remnant tower of Wren's neo-Gothic church of St Alban of 1685 to stand sentinel in the middle of the street. Royex House made a sad impression, with its mean ceiling heights, roughly cast concrete and a standard set of floor plates next to a lateral core. At the ground it was particularly antisocial, the entire Wood Street elevation being taken up by a ramp, part of the grand scheme of the Barbican high walk – a raised pedestrian system above the envisioned free-flowing lanes of cars. A back alley wove around this to connect the square

Eric Parry Architects, 5 Aldermanbury Square, London, 2007
View of 5 Aldermanbury Square from the northeast, looking across London Wall from the Barbican, with Basil Spence's Salters' Hall (1976) in the middle ground. The entasis of the east wing is exaggerated at the north corner by the acute angle of the street.

Eric Parry Architects, 5 Aldermanbury Square, London, 2007
The undercroft of 5 Aldermanbury Square connecting Wood Street (ahead) with the Square (behind). The soffit is made of polished granite to reflect the world below, while the space between the wings inclines to allow south light into the public area.

and street for the knowing. Coincidentally, prior to the commission for this building, due to be more than twice the height of 30 Finsbury Square which we had completed in 2002, I had written a short piece for the *Guardian* newspaper under their series titled 'Wonders and Blunders'. For the latter I happened to choose the Standard Chartered bank headquarters building in Aldermanbury Square, a mean pile of token stone facing and green powder-coated aluminium panels. For my 'wonder', I chose Edwin Lutyens's Cenotaph in Whitehall, previously described.

The brief for 5 Aldermanbury Square required it to be almost double the floor area of its 1960s predecessor while only being modestly higher. A number of spatial, perspectival and material ideas developed to allow the completed building to sit confidently but without dominating its neighbours. The first was to fragment the whole into three sections running north to south, the central one being recessed. The north of this section is occupied by the core of lifts and services and the public ramp is relocated to contemporary standards to the north curtilage of the building, thus liberating the Wood Street elevation. The recessed south of this section is curved downwards to allow sunlight to penetrate into the lower public areas now created to connect Wood Street to Aldermanbury Square lying to the east of the site. Next, because of the site configuration, a slippage of 6 metres (20 feet) between the east and west wings allowed the south facade to be less monumental. Whereas the horizontal emphasis of the 1960s building of solid spandrel panels with strip windows above makes an apparent doubling of the vertical layers (32 on the old 16 storeys), by reversing this to create a double-floor order encapsulating sections of two floors in one, the new 18-storey building is composed of nine vertical sections – 32 to 9.

This is possible because of the literal depth of the facade made by an exoskeletal structure of box sections at 6-metre (20-foot) centres, which are clad in shot-peened folded stainless-steel panels. At the structural grid these are stacked to appear as stainless-steel billets with connecting beams, rather than lintels between. At the non-structural 3-metre (10-foot) line a baffle is inserted, and at the intermediate levels an eyebrow independent of the framing elements creates shadow and acknowledges the intermediate floor.

To ease the verticality of the east and west flanks from the ninth level, the curve of the walls has a radius of 350 metres (1,150 feet) which creates the entasis of the whole, in fact faceted in two-storey sections but, like the example of the Parthenon, not noticeable without considerable concentration by the eye. The silk finish of the stainless-steel tapering responds to the sky and earth, further emphasising the mediation between the two. Finally from the pedestrian's perspective, the 35-metre- (115-foot-) wide soffit to the public realm, although 8 metres (26 feet) above the ground, could be a dark undercroft; but, paradoxically, by making this of polished black granite, it rather mysteriously inverts its presence through reflection to double the apparent height.

Bo Bardi, Kahn and Mies van der Rohe: Three Reflections on Architecture and Horizon

The Museu de Arte de São Paulo (MASP), outlined by Lina Bo Bardi in a single night and completed in 1968,[8] is a bold and uncompromised vision. Moreover, it signals the release of pent-up energy accumulated through a childhood and early adulthood spent in Italy and the new horizon opened to the architect in Brazil. Reflecting towards the end of her life on this radical shift she pursued after the end of the Second World War in 1945, Bo Bardi said:

> as a kid I was afraid of all the beauty in Rome and I said to myself 'why is everything in ruins? There must be an explanation'. When I arrived in Rio de

Lina Bo Bardi, Museu de Arte de São Paulo (MASP), São Paulo, Brazil, 1968
Aerial view of the museum, (right) which stands parallel to the Avenida Paulista and bridges the tunnel of the Avenida Nove de Julho. The principal exhibition spaces float — the suspension emphasized by the red of the superstructure — over the ground-level public terrace (left).

> Janeiro I met some amazing people … a group of intelligent and formidable young people, and on top of that there were no ruins in Rio. Everything was blue, very nice … what a marvel.[9]

The young Lina Bo's sense of old-world claustrophobia was no doubt intensified by the complexities of Italian politics, the deprivation of the war years, post-war occupation, maternal expectations of domestic diligence, and not least the male-dominated Italian architectural and design scene.

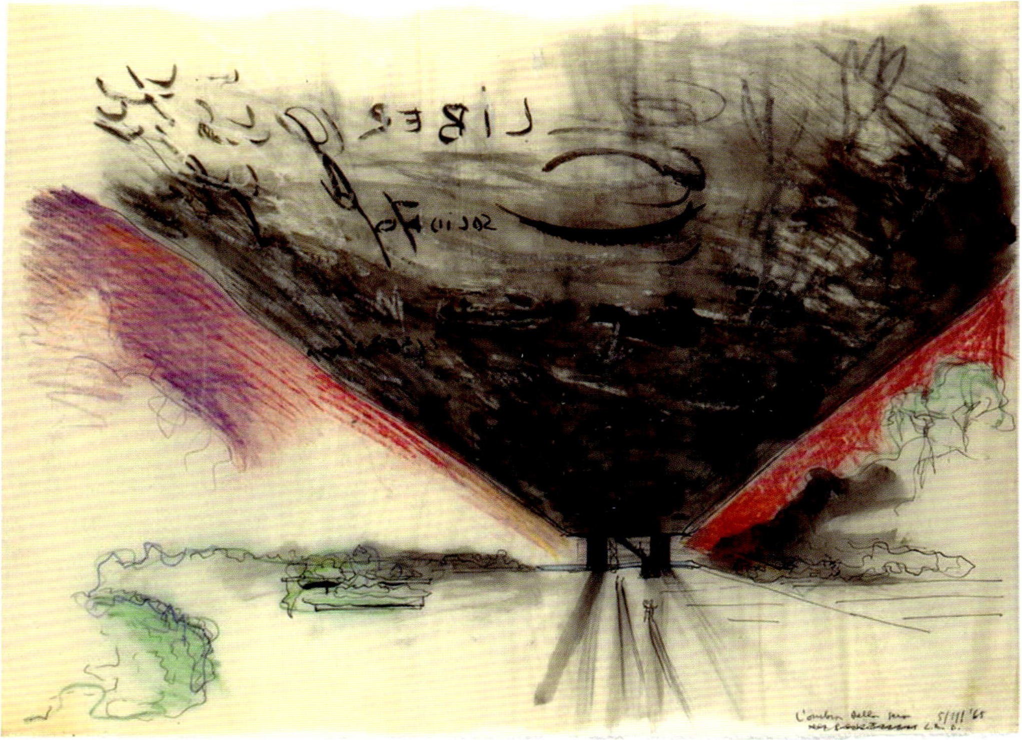

Lina Bo Bardi, Museu de Arte de São Paulo (MASP), São Paulo, Brazil, 1968: sketch of the undercroft
Inverted horizons: the soffit as earth, water pools into which the pillars are plunged as sky; celestial dancers inhabit the public space.

As an architectural student at La Sapienza university in Rome, she was instructed by Marcello Piacentini, the head of the school, and by Gustavo Giovannoni, whose intelligent approach to the palimpsest of new and old through *ambientismo* – a term he coined for a form of contextualism in restoration, rehabilitation and urban renewal which was historically and theoretically sourced – she admired. Piacentini was one of the Fascist regime's favoured architects and a prolific urban designer whose hand can be discerned in the reordering of many Italian cities. He was by the specific order of Benito Mussolini the leading designer and High Commissioner of the EUR (Esposizione Universale Roma), conceived as a model new city and the site of Rome's planned World's Fair in 1942. The plan and the design of the principal buildings were presented in a lavish leather-bound publication in 1938. The optimism of this and earlier town planning experiments like the reclamation project of Sabaudia set in the marshlands south of Rome, a new town centre built in less than a year following an architectural competition in 1933, must have filled the studios of La Sapienza during Lina Bo's time there. Italy was building during this short and intense period to a far more ambitious urban agenda than its European rivals, in spite of its oppressive political regime.

The openness of her new Brazilian horizon is exemplified by the manner in which she received the commission for the MASP. The building is sectionally tripartite: one aerial, double-stacked set of spaces; one subterranean set of interconnected levels; and the third part a void space between them. At the lower level, cut 9 metres (30 feet) into the ground below the Avenida Paulista, are two storeys of intertwined public rooms centred around a double-height public hall like a giant Baroque garden room. At the lowest level the hall is flanked by a library and a restaurant, while at the upper level around the hall are continuous exhibition spaces. A memorable red-painted concrete scissored stair connects the two levels and is the front-of-house parade to the nest of performance spaces set between the massive pillar legs of the superstructure. The stairs mark the long axis between the blind performance spaces and the frontal spaces overlooking the valley and the city beyond. The four piers/legs of the overarching body of the building hold, like the belly of a gymnast, the exhibition spaces dramatically suspended above the monumental public opening at street level. This opening to the city and horizon beyond is, in conformity with the stipulation of the gift of the land as a public belvedere, a space in radical contrast to the speculative development of the other plots bordering the Avenida. The space under the suspended exhibition rooms is a rectangular undercroft 70 by 29 metres (230 by 95 feet)

Lina Bo Bardi, Museu de Arte de São Paulo (MASP), São Paulo, Brazil, 1968
A concert taking place the undercroft.

with an extended area beyond forming the roof of the public rooms below. As an open-sided forum it has been the stage for political debate, fairs, market stalls, daily informal gatherings and a meeting place. More broadly it is a mediating point between the city and its cultural legacy.

Bo Bardi's MASP belongs to a small group of outstanding buildings that evolved in the aftermath of the Second World War, driven by philanthropy and a spirit of cultural communication rather than raw political ambition. The two other parallel exemplars I would suggest are Louis Kahn's Kimbell Art Museum in Fort Worth, Texas (1972) and Ludwig Mies van der Rohe's Neue Nationalgalerie in Berlin (1968). All three pursue a dialogue with horizon, albeit from radically different positions. Mies van der Rohe's experiments with an earthbound plinth and roof as a raised geological plane, with the continuous horizon achieved by the literal transparency of glass walls, began with his unbuilt project for a museum for a small city published in *Architectural Forum* in 1943[10] and followed by the Farnsworth House designed and built between 1945 and 1951. The work of Kahn's studio with perspective and the horizon as principal generator of space is

Lina Bo Bardi, Museu de Arte de São Paulo (MASP), São Paulo, Brazil, 1968
View of a permanent exhibition as originally designed and presented by Lina Bo Bardi. The paintings hang on glass panels set in concrete bases, which act as invisible easels. Bo Bardi's hang was as radical as the building itself.

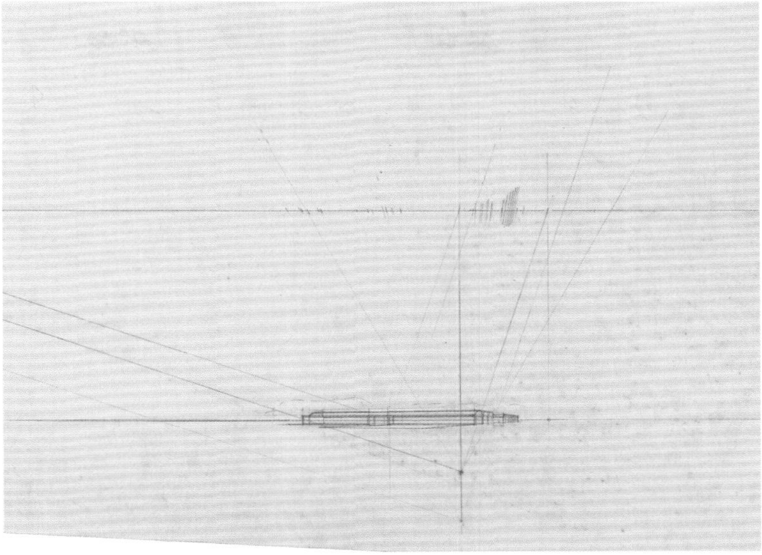

Louis Kahn, Kimbell Art Museum, Fort Worth, Texas: second perspectival drawing, 1967
Perspective framework drawing for Kahn's overlaid sketch studies. The viewpoint is set on the gently rising ground of the site from the southwest. The horizon line bisects the open entrance loggia. The bulk of the building is pressed into the ground as the vaults rise to admit light into the protective carapace.

epitomised by Kahn's well-known teachings on the power of architecture and its philosophical horizons. The Kimbell Art Museum evolved as a balance between the subterranean below the horizon and the equivalent of frame and wall above, capturing light from the propped gap between the cast concrete vault beams. The inverse of Mies's literal transparency, Kahn's Kimbell walls provide a continuity of massive material from exterior to interior that draws with it the presence of horizon.

Multiple Horizons

The question of where the datum lies is one that a designer immediately faces when thinking about the sectional qualities of a building or landscape. A landscape designer approximates the characteristics of topography against the measure of their own body to establish the 'lie' of the land and the paths that the flow of water over its surfaces will take. An architect thinks about the way a level relates to its surrounding spaces and the nominal horizontal line from which things rise above and sink below.

In 2001, faced with a competition to design a new and important social and academic complex for the Bocconi university in Milan, which required a massive quantum of space on a restricted urban site, a member of the Grafton

Grafton Architects, Università Commerciale Luigi Bocconi, School of Economics, Milan, Italy: initial sketch, 2001
A sketch annotated 'Datum? No datum?', indicating the floating masses of the office wings, separated to allow light into the liberated levels below with the topography of an ambiguous or multiple horizon of ground and lower-ground levels.

Architects team poignantly sketched and penned a note 'Datum? No Datum?', and with dotted lines suggested a solution of multiple principal levels.

The Università Commerciale Luigi Bocconi in Milan is one of Italy's leading universities, specialising in the fields of business, economics, law and the social sciences – an equivalent to the London School of Economics in the UK. Founded in 1902, it was unfettered by a nostalgia for any historic physical roots, and in 1941 (with a generous endowment from Benito Mussolini) it moved campus in order to be able to expand, employing Giuseppe Pagano

Grafton Architects, Università Commerciale Luigi Bocconi, School of Economics, Milan, Italy, 2008
View from the stair rising into the Aula Magna, the soffit of which pitches upwards dramatically to reveal the city through the glass wall at street level.

Grafton Architects, Università Commerciale Luigi Bocconi, School of Economics, Milan, Italy, 2008
Exterior view of the overlapping glass scales that dematerialise the walls.

to design the first university building containing offices, student common rooms and lecture spaces – a university hub in a series of interlocking finely proportioned wings connected by a central spine. The building echoes Walter Gropius's Bauhaus in Dessau, Germany, completed in 1925, the most progressive Modern Movement pedagogic building of its time. The interior of Pagano's building is also close in spirit to those of his contemporary Giuseppe Terragni's Casa del Fascio in Como (1936). I dwell on this first building because Grafton Architects' recent 'Cuore di Cristallo per Milano' ('Crystal Heart for Milan') echoes aspects of its relatively small neighbour and forebear, particularly in the structure of wings.

The competition brief called for a dramatic density of use: 883 offices, a 1,000-seat auditorium – the Aula Magna with adjacent foyers, conference facilities and smaller lecture spaces – and parking for 190 cars. The challenge was to accommodate the brief on a rectangular site 60 by 180 metres (200 by 600 feet) with height restrictions in conformity with the housing opposite on Via Röntgen, and more importantly to devise a spatial idea that would allow the openness of community, both student and city, while respecting the quietude of individual study.

To do this, Grafton Architects developed a section that allowed the city ground plane at street level to continue across the entire site, punctuated by the volume of the Aula Magna, the structural piers, stairs and lifts and a

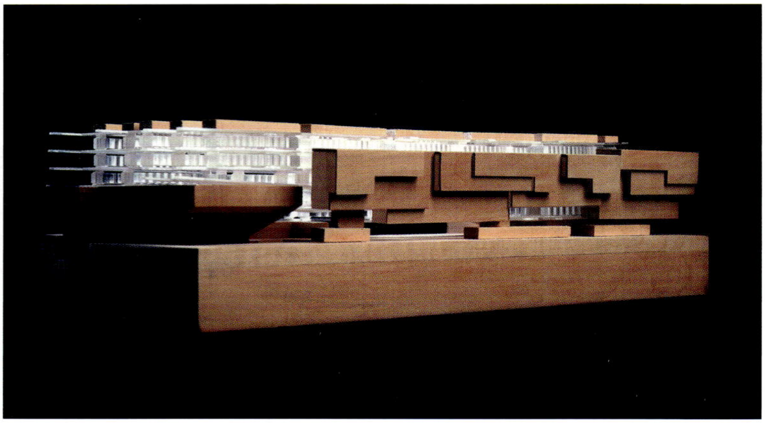

minimum of service spaces. Levitated just over 5 metres (16 feet) above street level, giving a clear minimum soffit level of over 4 metres (13 feet), are five floors of offices, part rising to six. These are arranged in serried bars, seven offices abreast, offset to avoid interminable or double-loaded corridors. Voids of 6 metres (20 feet) and more separate opposing offices and are external. The typical upper-floor plans have the precision of a military formation drilled by the taught structural logic of the piers that rise to form twin wall beams 3.4 metres (11 feet) apart that support the massive roof-level beams. These span 24 metres (80 feet) – the dimension of seven offices – from which all the floors are suspended by steel tendons.

The post-tensioned roof beams and floor slabs had phases of tensioning during construction to avoid creep, as did the floor-supporting vertical tendons – like a grand piano around its frame. All the piers are collected on a massive raft 2 to 3 metres (6 to 10 feet) thick, 17 metres (55 feet) below street level and contained by a concrete box because the bottom 7 metres (23 feet) of the box sit below the water table. The visible concrete is mainly self-compacting to achieve the standard of finish required. The structural clarity was the brainchild of Emilio Pereira, responding to spatial logic required by the architects. The liberation of the street plane thus achieved, a second public level was created 5.3 metres (17 feet 5 inches) below, cleverly open but at the same time separated from the everyday world of the city. This lower public space anchors the floating mass of 1,000 rooms above and is wrapped, as if by a giant clerestory, by the perimeter walls of glass. The Aula Magna rises through the ground plane like the palate of a whale at the critical intersection of the two surrounding streets, the Via Röntgen and Viale

Grafton Architects, Università Commerciale Luigi Bocconi, School of Economics, Milan, Italy, 2008
The aerial photo (right) shows the School of Economics at number 7, forming the 'Cyrstal Heart of the City' in its central city location; the model of the office wings (left) illustrates the overlapping glass scales that dematerialise the walls of the school of economics, giving a translucent light to the interior, while reflecting light, ultimately, to the ground and lower ground levels.

Bligny. The architects have described the project as like an oyster: 'A tough grey carapace on the outside, but white, light and delicate on the inside.'[11]

Shelley McNamara and Yvonne Farrell, directors of Grafton Architects, have an instinct for the subterranean and the aerial which is powerfully manifest in their built work. In earlier projects like their townhouse in Denzille Lane, Dublin (1998), with planks of floating glass in its extension volume, there is a premonition of the glazed skin of the upper office wings at Bocconi; while at the Department of Mechanical and Manufacturing Engineering for Trinity College Dublin (1996), which employs the device of semi-basement-level top-lit workshops in order to subjugate the mass of the building on its sensitive historic site without losing sight of their character and presence, the seeds are sown for the sunken public realm at Bocconi. And since the completion of their Milan building, their education buildings for the School of Economics at the Université Toulouse 1 Capitole in France (under construction) have employed similar devices for the separation of the public and semi-public realms. They have also, in exhibition designs at the 2012 Venice Architecture Biennale and most recently in their installation at the 'Sensing Spaces' exhibition at London's Royal Academy of Arts in early 2014, explored the material corollaries of the dark–light, earth–air metaphor.

Grafton Architects, Università Commerciale Luigi Bocconi, School of Economics, Milan, Italy, 2008
Model (top) and elevation of the School of Economics on the Viale Bligny. The striking sculptural form of the main elevation of the institution gives it a strong identity and presence on this busy urban thoroughfare.

This chapter opened with the marking of the horizon as a means of communicating with its eternal presence. Through historical time, the underlying urge has metamorphosed into the representation of the city and its skyline in a confusion of individual and collective representation. The question of wellbeing and horizon was articulated through examples of projection, perspective and optical refinement. Lately in the 20th century the expanding capacity of structures has enabled the relative liberation of the ground place, a success abused in a litany of urban disasters in parallel with the outstandingly good examples cited. The question of the adjacency of parts within a larger entity draws us to the next chapter that develops around the idea of simultaneity.

References

1. Cornelius A van Peursen, 'The Horizon', in FA Elliston and P McCormick (eds), *Husserl: Expositions and Appraisals*, University of Notre Dame Press (Notre Dame, IN and London), 1977, p 185.
2. Quoted in Michel Fraisset, *Atelier de Cézanne*, Éditions aux Arts (Aix-en-Provence), undated, p 33.
3. Joseph von Planta, 'An Account of the Romansh Language, by Joseph Planta, FRS, in a Letter to Sir John Pringle, Bart. PRS', *Philosophical Transactions of the Royal Society of London*, vol 66, 1776, pp 129–59, http://www.jstor.org/stable/106271, (accessed June 2013).
4. *Ibid* pp 144–5.
5. Mario Morini, *Atlante di Storia Dell'Urbanistica*, Ulrico Hoepli (Milan), 1963.
6. For example: Albert d'Haenens, *Europe of the North Sea and the Baltic: The World of the Hanse*, Fonds Mercator (Antwerp), 1984.
7. Le Corbusier, *Towards a New Architecture* [*Vers une architecture*, 1923], Architectural Press (London), 1946, pp 185–207.
8. Olívia de Oliveira, 'Interview with Lina Bo Bardi' (1991), Olívia de Oliveira, *Lina Bo Bardi / Obra construída / Built Work*, 2G / Editorial Gustavo Gili (Barcelona), 2002, p 244.
9. *Ibid* p 230.
10. *New Buildings for 194X*, special issue of *Architectural Forum*, vol 78, no 5, May 1943.
11. Interview by Catherine Slessor with Yvonne Farrell and Shelley McNamara, quoted in *Architectural Review*, 1 March 2009.

3 Simultaneity

No idea, apart perhaps from the specificity of place, is more central to context than that of simultaneity. Simultaneity is the cumulative effect of related parts to a spatial configuration. The notion of simultaneity can be applied both to the apparently limited field of a picture – think for instance of a Cubist composition, depicting objects from more than one viewpoint in a single image – or to the complex scale of a city, as in the case of London explored in the latter part of this chapter. Architecturally the framework within which we can begin to appreciate the simultaneity of parts is most usefully understood through the notion of typical situations.

A typical situation is a means of understanding the normative condition of living for which architectural space provides a setting, be it sleeping, eating, working or studying, to mention a few. Dalibor Vesely has established the ground for an interpretation of space that subverts the trajectory of technological thinking; as he puts it, 'complexity can be produced, but richness must be created'.[1] Citing the case of the Eiffel Tower, he illustrates lucidly how the distance between its abstract form and the richness of Parisian culture was only bridged by way of its acceptance and transcendence through its cultural manifestation in film, literature and art.

This chapter is organised in an ascending scale of spaces as a means of suggesting the applicability of the idea of simultaneity to context. Like Georges Perec's *Species of Spaces* (1974),[2] which begins with his bed 'that the bailiffs don't have the power to seize' and travels from Paris's 16th arrondissement to Europe and the universe, we begin at the scale of a room with Sigmund Freud's study and consulting room. Next a house: the first radical use of iron in a domestic setting in Victor Horta's Hôtel Tassel; and then to the scale of a housing estate, the Golden Lane Estate in London. Beyond the estate, we examine the simultaneity that creates a complex layering for a city quarter on the edge of Trafalgar Square, focusing on the surroundings of the Church of St Martin-in-the-Fields, London, and then turn in passing to the reciprocity of Trafalgar Square and other London centres that make up a contemporary mapping.

Room

In May 1938 the 31-year-old photographer Edmund Engelman was contacted by August Aichhorn, one of the circle of Viennese psychoanalysts close to the movement's founder Sigmund Freud, and asked if he would undertake the commission to make a photographic record of Freud's home and office. Simmering disdain in Vienna had become open harassment by the Nazi authorities, and finally Freud and his close family had been given permission to leave for exile in England; the historical context for his life and work were therefore about to be dismantled.

Over a period of days, without the use of flash which would have alerted the Gestapo observers, and doing his best to avoid disturbing Freud (aided by Aichhorn's close reading of his daily routine), Engelman completed his task. Engelman had himself to flee to the USA in 1939 and after the war tracked down his negatives which had by then been sent to England, so it is most poignant that we are able to share the intensity of Freud's private world. Berggasse, meaning 'Mountain Alley', is a street in a district of Vienna north of the historic city, the Innere Stadt, and separated by the Ringstrasse, but close to the University of Vienna's medical departments, museum and hospital. Freud had lived in the same building for 47 years. Here Sigmund and Martha brought up a family and Sigmund analysed most of his patients, corresponded with the world at large, wrote most of his books, and met with his associates and visitors – a veritable who's who of intellectual and literary European culture. To anyone interested particularly in the history of design, the haut-bourgeois apartment holds little; it almost entirely eschews the fashions that vociferously engulfed Vienna during the concurrent half century. The steady accumulation of artefacts are a testimony to Freud's weekly round of visits to antiquarian dealers; there are no interesting spatial adjustments to the existing building and no evidence of contemporary visual arts.

The family apartment and Freud's office are approached through the building towards the courtyard garden. Lit from the courtyard, the common stair of the building, a miniature version of the *Treppenhalle* (stair hall) of Baroque Viennese palaces, is reached via four steps ascending from the slurry of the street, which give access to a landing and thence to the stone risers of the dog-leg flights to each floor above. At the first floor a door to the left was the entry to the family apartment, with formal sitting rooms overlooking the street, an internal kitchen with ventilation and some light from a lightwell, and the bedrooms facing the urban block interior. The door to the right, signed 'Prof Dr Freud 3–4' (being his visiting hours), opened into a foyer, with Anna Freud's consulting room accessed through her bedroom to the street, while Sigmund Freud's consulting room and study was accessed from a common waiting room facing the quiet of the courtyard. From the waiting

Berggasse, Vienna, photographed in May 1938
The Freud family occupied the apartment in the left-hand portion of the first floor of number 19 Berggasse, in the middle of the picture, from 1891 to 1938. The image is part of Edmund Engelman's photographic study of the apartment, made shortly before the Freuds went into exile in London.

room, the analysand was ushered to Freud's study and then to the day bed in the consulting room, at the head of which, at right angles to the axis of the day bed, were Freud's armchair and ottoman stool. While Engelman did not photograph the topography from Freud's point of view, it is fascinating to ponder the resonant landscape as seen from his mind's eye, through Engelman's photographs and aided by Rita Ransohoff's captions.[3]

Hovering above Freud's right shoulder was the ghostly life-size portrait of an unidentified Roman, representative of citizenship and order. On the walls either side of the corner a set of horizons were established. The middle of these involved everyday and zoomorphic themes, with contemporary drawings of comic encounter by Wilhelm Busch, fragments of painted stucco illustrating a sphinx, Silenus, lions, a pelican, a flamingo, a grotesque mask and an illustration of a proto-Ionic capital. The upper level was dominated by two-layer painted stucco fragments of a centaur and Pan, the phallic-pleasure-seeking ego. The lower order, set at Freud's sitting eye level, consisted of a papyrus fragment illustrating the Egyptian gods of the underworld Horus, Anubis and Osiris and set at the same height as a table top crowded with Egyptian wooden funerary figures. The Turkish carpets bedecking the day bed, the wall and the floor were notably reminiscent of a tribal nomadic tent exotically patterned and coloured by the dyes of nature that, settled in whatever rugged context, represented the order of a paradisiacal garden. On the wall above the day bed was a framed photograph of the 13th-century-BC cliff-hewn statues of Ramses II at Abu Simbel in southern Egypt, presumably hung to represent the continuity of past and present.

Looking to his left, Freud would have had a foreshortened view of the analysand's head and body quivering through vocal stirrings. Above the analysand's feet and framing the wall hanging were a copy of Ingres's *Oedipus and the Sphinx* (1808) and a high relief of an approaching ambulant Gradiva.

At the upper register directly above Freud's head was a painted bearded portrait of Roman period that bore a resemblance to a youthful Freud. Mirroring this portrait was a photograph of an admired colleague, Ernst von Fleischl-Marxow – a man Freud said he was happy to take as a model.[4] Across the room on a short section of wall between window and door hung a reproduction of André Brouillet's *Une Leçon clinique à la Salpêtrière* (1887), which depicts a lesson given by Dr Charcot, under whom Freud had studied in Paris and for whom he had an enduring regard. And so floating

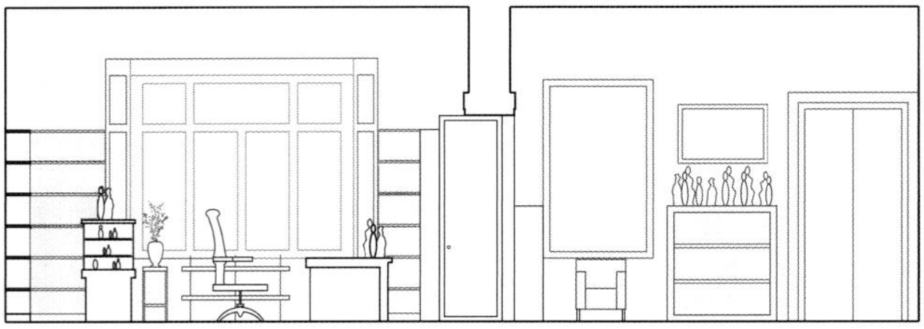

Section A-A′

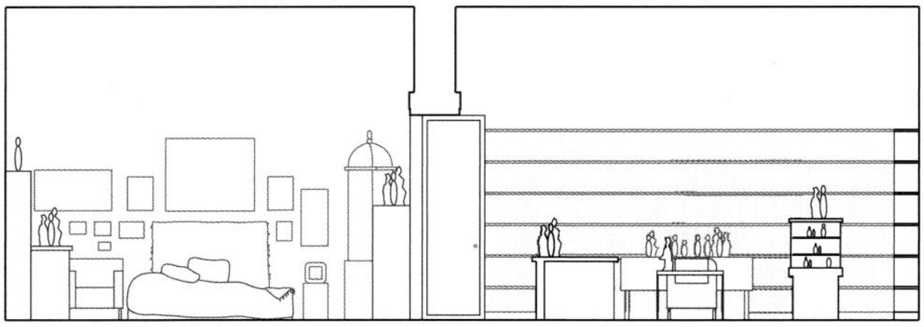

Section B-B′

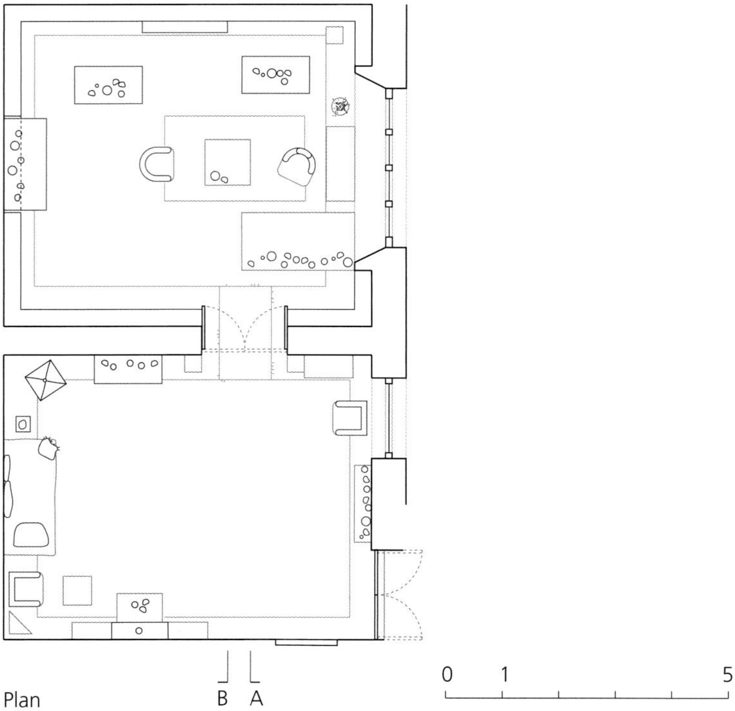

Plan

Eric Parry Architects, reconstructed plan and sections of the Freud family apartment, 19 Berggasse, Vienna, 2013
Based on Edmund Engelman's May 1938 photographic study, the plan and sections show Sigmund Freud's interconnecting study and consulting room.

Sigmund Freud's consulting room and study at 19 Berggasse, Vienna, photographed in May 1938
View of Freud's corner fauteuil and ottoman, with the analysand's couch in the foreground.

at this upper register was a private pantheon. As a student, Freud had had a fantasy that one day his own bust would sit among those of former illustrious professors at the University of Vienna and that on it would be quoted a line from Sophocles' 5th-century BC play *Oedipus Tyrannus*: 'who divined the famed riddle and was a man most mighty'.[5]

The resonances continued in abundance, with the cabinet of winged figures and that of vessels and containers flanking the door to his book-lined study, and his writing table, at which the sequence found a culminating reflective intensity, lightened by the enigmatic smile of the figure of a Chinese scholar whom Freud is said to have greeted each day when he came into his study.

The mnemonic layering of domestic space is absolutely common to humankind: the household *lares* (statues representing protective gods) of the ancient city have been replaced by shelves of nick-nacks and photographs of family and friends, but the apartment at 19 Berggasse remains, for obvious reasons, an epic of its kind.

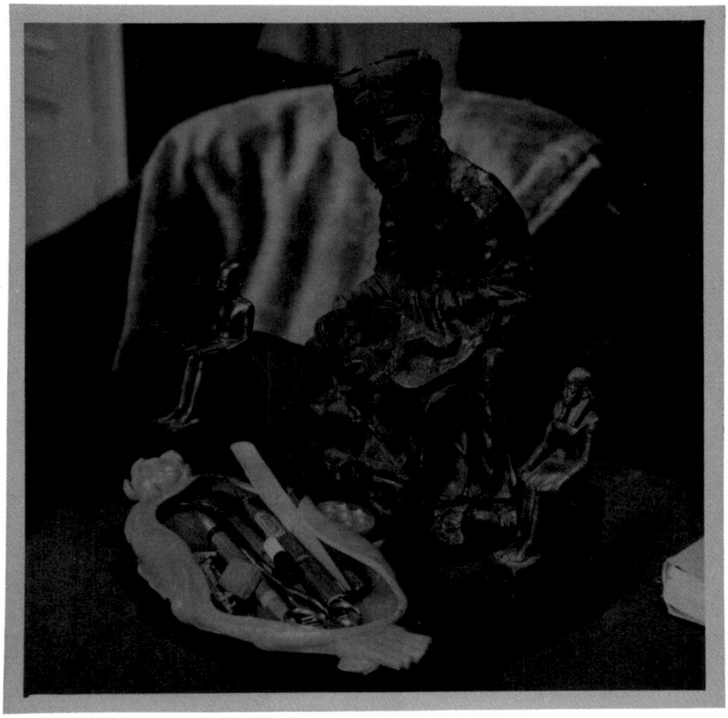

Sigmund Freud's consulting room and study at 19 Berggasse, Vienna, photographed in May 1938
Figurine of a Chinese scholar, guardian Egyptian gods and implements: Freud's *lararium* at the corner of his desk.

In terms of the relationship between the domestic urban interior and the city, the apartment buildings of central Europe, the burgher town houses of the Low Countries and the Baltic and the terraced houses of England are as spatially different as the literature and broader urban culture of which they are a part. From Charles Dickens in the 19th century to Zadie Smith in the 21st, English literature is littered with front doors to the street, while entire German novels unwind around the common stair of apartment buildings such as Hans Fallada's *Alone in Berlin* (1947) or Uwe Timm's *The Invention of Curried Sausage* (1993). The merchants of northern Europe developed a hybrid, a deep-planned building with a public sphere at ground level and with domestic rooms above, epitomised in Thomas Mann's novel *Buddenbrooks* (1901).

The apartment and the house are naturally as different as landscape and portrait proportions of pictures. Freud's apartment is a complex grouping of rooms set at one level, with the height, width and framing details of openings signifying a latent domestic hierarchy of formal and informal entrances and exits.

House

The organisation of a town house on a restricted plot width isolates the rooms at each level from each other; an entrance lobby is elongated into a passage, and the shared lightwell that allows a deep plan to function in an apartment building is no longer viable. With larger street frontages, L-shaped plans with deep extensions produced inventive architectural enfilades of rooms developed to heightened degrees of sophistication in 18th- and 19th-century European cities.

The use of the iron frame in domestic architecture to liberate spatial relationships up till then restricted by load-bearing masonry was sudden and sensational. The domestic stage, which had been axial and restricted with the exception of stair halls, became active in three dimensions, offering not only the diagonal views but also the openness and interrelationship of stacked spaces.

The difference is immediately apparent when a comparison is drawn between 19 Berggasse and plans of the Hôtel Solvay and the Hôtel van Eetvelde in Brussels, both designed by Victor Horta in the mid-1890s and completed in 1900. The Hôtels Solvay and van Eetvelde are subsequent to a smaller experiment by Horta, the Hôtel Tassel, designed in 1892 and completed in 1894. It was the product of two trajectories: firstly the architect's personal journey and secondly the culture of *fin-de-siècle* Brussels. Horta was born in 1861, just 31 years after the Kingdom of Belgium was established in the uncertainty of post-Napoleonic Europe. From the age of 12 he studied music at the Conservatory in his hometown Ghent, where he began his architectural training in 1876. He lived and worked in Paris for two years before returning to Belgium and continuing his training at the Académie des Beaux-Arts in Brussels. There, he was taught by Alphonse Balat, architect to Leopold II and designer of the botanical hothouses at Laeken from which Horta observed and absorbed the possibilities of riveted metal frame construction, wrought iron and glass, materials that were to become so overt in his domestic interiors.

The urban context had been established for these seminal projects by the developments directed by Brussels's *bourgmestre* Jules Victor Anspach (1829–1879), which paralleled those of Baron Haussmann in Paris (see Chapter 4). They included the creation of boulevards that encircled the old city, like many other European examples. Lining the boulevards were not wide-fronted apartment blocks, which proved unpopular, but narrow plots

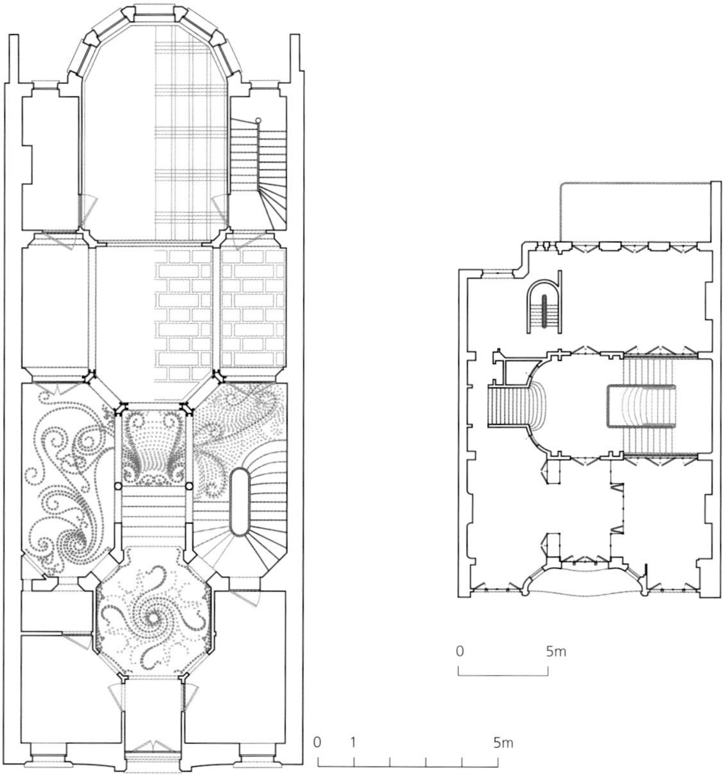

Eric Parry Architects, comparative plans of two Brussels buildings by Victor Horta, 2013
On the left is the ground floor of the Hôtel Tassel (1894), showing its pavement. A terraced house captured between party walls, it was nevertheless radically opened to the diagonal, both in plan and section. On the right is the first floor of the later Hôtel Solvay (1900), showing its folding screens.

for development as single town houses. The plot on which the Hôtel Tassel stands is 27 metres (89 feet) long by 7.8 metres (23 feet) wide, and the plan of the house itself is 21 metres (69 feet) long, subjugating the rear court to a mere 6 metres (20 feet) and creating the constraints from which Horta's brilliant internal artificial garden emerged. Horta recalled, in the spirit of the Symbolist movement that this was a time when, 'synthesising my thought, I declared that the house should not only be in the image of the occupant's life, it should be the very "portrait" of it!'[6]

The client, Émile Tassel, was an engineer, professor of descriptive geometry, research fellow of the Solvay Society and fascinated by optics and photography. Unencumbered by the needs of a family, he was a well-known Freemason, a bachelor devoted to his grandmother who lived in the house with him. The house is principally the transformation of the bourgeois family residence into a crossover between monumental residence, academic club and laboratory. The facade reflects the unorthodox vertical hierarchy of the street-facing rooms. The central bay of the elevation dominates, occupying almost half the width of the plot, with the double-storey bay window providing a focus. The lower section of the bay, marked by five diminutive and primitively ordered columns in front of the stained-glass windows to a mezzanine room, have the physiognomy of a sanctuary. On the floor above the projecting bay is Tassel's private studio and optics laboratory, whose tripartite window affords an enormous area of glazing to the room which is

Victor Horta, Hôtel Tassel, Brussels, 1894: lightwell and main stair
The top-lit stair of the Hôtel Tassel, showing Victor Horta's liberation of the domestic interior through the use of the iron frame.

physically removed from the house by the enclosed passage and the flight of steps that approach it. The nuances and subtlety of this facade, ranging from its emphasis on solidity in the small flanking windows to the exaggerated transparency of the central bay horizontally and the compressions and expansions vertically, reflecting the order of the section and uses behind, are of the highest compositional and material skill. It speaks to a rich tradition of merchant houses in the public realm while manifesting the radical reinterpretation of the interior architecture.

Passing through the vestibule, we enter an octagonal space with the last vestiges of load-bearing masonry, with alternating long and short faces. The floor level is 1 metre (3 feet) lower than the general level of the floor that recedes 15 metres (50 feet) beyond the rear bay window. It is a place of initiation; the white tessellated marble mosaic is set radially from the central brass disk, from which mosaic flames in orange and red gyrate.

The six steps leading out of the octagonal vestibule are generous and open; here the ambiguity and views of the entrance are gone and there is a rigorous

Eric Parry and David Dernie, section through the lightwell and main stair of Victor Horta's Hôtel Tassel in Brussels, 1985
Sectional elevation, with canted plan, of the entry sequence to the Hôtel Tassel. Survey and drawing immediately following its restoration from boarding house decay.

invisible axis, established longitudinally through the house, across which the spaces weave symmetrically. The first of these spaces is the lightwell bay itself, opening on both sides of the steps, over which a double-curved vault rises and falls.

The vault is edged by a curving composite steel beam reminiscent of the steel bressumer built into the facade. This beam is supported on a filigree dosseret which emerges from the 'budding' capital of a painted cast-iron column with gilded relief. To the left of this vaulted passage is the winter garden, the floor of which is one step lower. The ribbed patent glazing of the skylight follows the curve of the passage beam. The party wall is mirrored from above eye level to the underside of the skylight and reflects the stairwell on the opposite party wall, itself naturally lit through a laylight at first-floor ceiling level. The winter garden, which was furnished with bamboo chairs, tables and pedestals for exotic tropical plants mingling with the metalwork and wall decoration, is reflected by the stairwell mural washed in natural light. This central mural has a subtle gradation of tone that reinforces the penetration of the natural light, and establishes the illusion of spatial depth set against the colour and tone of the complex stylised Art Nouveau line.

The lightwell bay is the equivalent of a *cour d'honneur*: the salon looks on to it and not to the street. Every element in the space – whether paint, mosaic, metal balustrade, light fitting, column or beam – echoes another in the synthesis of a symphonic poem. This silent and static space is sealed from the outside world by obscured glass and the surrounding building; it is an exquisite, concrete example of the Symbolist's vision of an 'artificial paradise'.

The internal facade of the lightwell bay, unlike the solidity and decorum of the street facade, is a five-bay steel structure, whose piers are hollow trapezoids made of composite steel sections. These piers, measuring 450 by 170 millimetres (17¾ by 6¾ inches), are used to change the direction of the spatial geometry in a masterful way with directional shifts, also orchestrating the changing hierarchical order of the spaces: passage, central bay of the salon, culminating in the dining room which overlooks the garden.

The main stair in the southwest lightwell is a geometrical construction of considerable complexity: of its 26 treads, only six are perpendicular to its main axis. To both the client, Tassel, professor of descriptive geometry, and the architect Horta, who perhaps was taught by him, this stair must have given great pleasure. Here, where elegance is paramount, the stair ascends with the most grace. The first steps emerge from the ground as the handrail and balustrade peel away from the straight wall. The steps are then visually absorbed by the stringer, and the shapes left between the curvilinear wrought-iron balustrade hemmed in by the handrail are echoed by the freer spirit and material of those on the mural. The stair is apparently floating, emphasised by the tendril bracket which appears almost to be holding it down.

The wrought-iron balustrade is fabricated from metal strips of equal width but different thicknesses (9 and 6.4 millimetres (⅜ and ¼ inch), and for some of the more complex configurations, 3 millimetres (⅛ inch)). These strips are bent, their ends drawn or thickened, and riveted together. Horta, obsessed by the 'correct' placing of rivets, used many different configurations; the diameter of the heads of the rivets holding the decorative sheet at the junction of the piers to beams in the salon is 30 millimetres (1⅛ inches), while those used on the balustrade measure a more conventional 10 millimetres (⅜ inch). A rivet is never used to strengthen two parallel strips by fixing them together. Instead the balustrade is a series of discontinuous moving elements fixed at the moment of their meeting by the rivets, which appear like water droplets whose surface tension is stretched to the limit and caught at that instant by the photographic image. The balustrading is not painted in the even way that other metal elements are: the white primer is visible through the dragged top coat, and what might be mistaken for worn paintwork on a rivet head or the hard edge is in fact a carefully considered expression of the form.

The Hôtel Tassel is a brilliant illustration of the – admittedly extreme – synthesis of parts to a whole, and it is easy to mistake the achievement at its date. In plan and section, the opening of diagonal and complex sequences in three dimensions provided a rich spatial topography for the exploration of simultaneity, a precursor to the pictorial experiments of the Fauves and Cubists in the early years of the 20th century.

Moving from the room and then the house as we have, the architecture of multiple dwellings develops from the concerns of the interior to the shared territory of external space. Between the archetypes of the street and the square lies the vexed question of the urban block, its scale massing, proximities and character. While historic urban fabric has proved to be flexible in the fluctuation of living requirements, at a certain point the grand floor-to-ceiling heights and the formality of large rooms limit the density of affordable inhabitation.

Estate

Given the depth of research and implementation of some excellent examples of mid- to high-density urban housing in Europe in the half century between 1890 and 1940 and then again in the post-war period, the extraordinary complacency with which the terrible state of housing is now accepted seems highly negligent, if not criminal. The current laissez-faire political response is strikingly similar to the situation in the 1950s where the quantum of new housing annually led to social entrapment and stigmatisation of generations in sink estates in most UK cities. There is little relief to the turgid crassness of recent housing design seen from any train journey around the country, and the arid quality of the space between buildings and in shared communal territories – the subject of the simultaneity of parts – is equally shocking, to the extent that when a good project like Accordia in Cambridge (built between 2003 and 2011 to designs by Feilden Clegg Bradley Studios, MaccreanorLavington and Alison Brooks Architects) turns up it is received with deep collective relief.

The private leafy estate in an affluent city is not, however, a reasonable benchmark. It is salutary to return to a housing estate conceived in the post-war crisis that really does work, and to analyse why. The Golden Lane Estate has 1,400 dwellings and marks the northern boundary of the City of London. I remember as a student of architecture in the early 1970s studying problematic local authority housing schemes in Newcastle upon Tyne, Glasgow, Manchester and London. At the time, two schemes seemed full of promise. The first was the Byker Wall designed by Ralph Erskine, then under construction in Newcastle and conspicuous for the unusually open consultation process, with the architect's satellite office as the site for this purpose as well as for the coordination of the design with the local executive architect. The second was the Golden Lane Estate (1962), where the composition of buildings and landscape left a deep impression of an exciting sequential experience. Writing just a few years after the latter's completion, Ian Nairn in his intensely personal London guide described it well:

> The buildings themselves – a very high-density housing estate for the City of London – are sometimes fussy and sometimes weather beaten. But in a way they are unimportant compared to the spaces between them ... There are half a dozen ways of crossing the site: along corridors, under buildings, down steps and up ramps. And it is all meant to be used. The space itself, continually fluctuating and flickering, new views always opening and faster than the eye

> can take them in … There is a new Peabody Estate next door: tall blocks, asphalt between, and a list of prohibitions as long as your arm. It is difficult to credit that it is intended for the same species of animal.[7]

What Nairn instinctively grasped was the generous combination of social and community spaces that are able to serve both the estate and the wider community.

The bomb-ravaged site, the clearance of which was reckoned to require three years' work, was pitted by deep basements that had been part of the workshops and warehouses of London's rag trade.

The brief was based on the City of London's need to house its key workers in closer proximity than on its outlying estates and was formulated as an open competition in 1951–2, which attracted 178 entries. Geoffry Powell's entry won, and the young practice of Chamberlin, Powell and Bon was established, the other two partners-to-be having submitted their own unsuccessful entries. The competition scheme improved hugely with development and the

Chamberlin, Powell and Bon, Golden Lane Estate, London, 1962: view from one of the buildings
Residents' diagonal view from the southeast towards the northwest corner of the Golden Lane Estate. In the middle lies the public swimming pool. and beyond the covered way are the estate tennis courts.

addition of adjacent land, but the skeleton, particularly of the landscape and disposition of key spaces by the placing of blocks, is clearly evident from the drawings and occasional comments in books and journals, such as 'What I am concerned with is the design of a group of buildings in close proximity to each other as if they were a single problem in design'[8] and 'We strongly dislike the garden city tradition with its low density, monotony and waste of good country, roads, curbs, borders, paths in endless strips everywhere.'[9]

The site was almost square, measuring 170 by 150 metres (560 by 490 feet). Two principal axes define its order: one north–south, passing from Fann Street through the 'bastion', a rugged-landscaped truncated core; the other east–west, passing through the 16-storey Great Arthur House from Goswell Road to Golden Lane.

The two most forcefully singular buildings are Crescent House (completed 1962) marking Goswell Road, the last building designed and a precursor of the concrete tectonic of the later Barbican development nearby; while the pivotal tower marking the gravitational centre of the scheme was Great Arthur House (completed 1959). Behind, or east of Crescent House, whose flats face east–west, six separated building bars, all with living rooms facing south and with deck access from the north, provide the 'warp' of the weave of landscape and communal buildings. The 'weft' is provided by the lower boundary building to Golden Lane, Stanley Cohen House; the axis of the community centre and Great Arthur House; the two-storey domino-like construction containing the swimming pool and badminton court; and, to the west, Crescent House.

Lifting the buildings off the plan provides an interesting dissection revealing the communal structure of the ground and lower-ground planes. The western edge of Goswell Road is a busy street leading directly southwards to the city and, fittingly, below the apartments at street level seemingly inspired by Le Corbusier's Maisons Jaoul in Paris (1956), but crammed with shops, cafés, a hardware store, opticians and hairstylists. To the south the colonnade opens up and is terminated by the Shakespeare pub. They are serviced from the lower-ground level, which is encircled by the gardens of the lower-ground studio apartments of Hatfield House. To the north a series of play spaces, a tenants' hall and changing rooms for the pool lead south to the two open tennis courts, initially designated as a bowling green. The bar containing the swimming pool has at its northern end a nursery/playschool and an external space used as a miniature allotment created out of construction site skip bags.

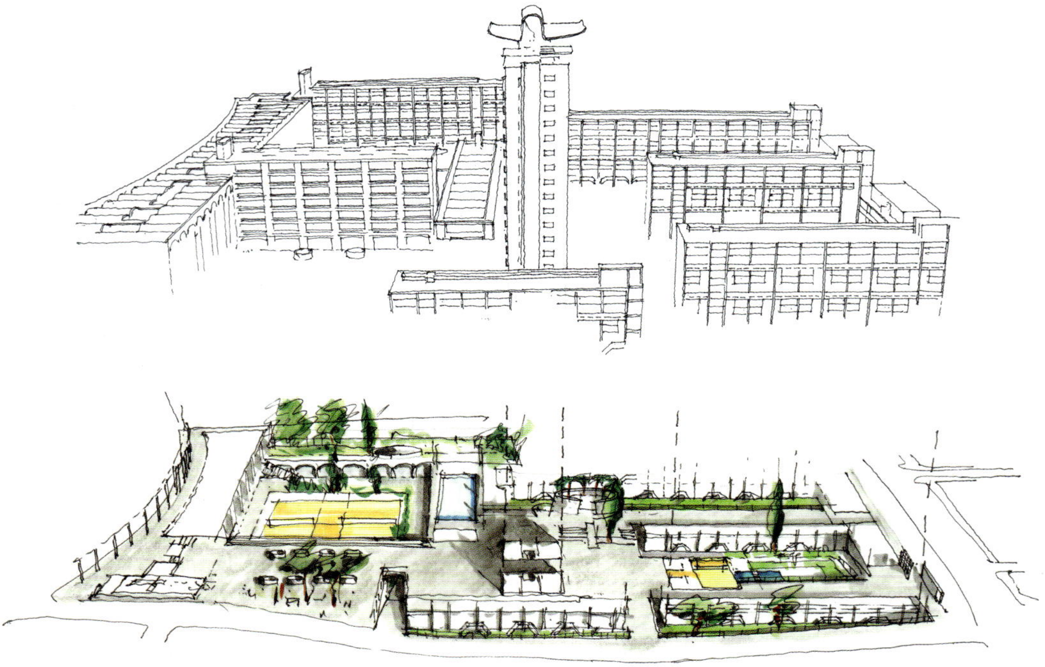

Eric Parry, perspective sketch of Chamberlin, Powell and Bon's Golden Lane Estate, 2014
Sketch of the ground and lower-ground levels showing the community centre, swimming pool and sports club, tennis courts, shopping arcade and pub.

Under Great Arthur House is the estate office which also, given the small size of the maisonettes and flats (58 square metres (620 square feet) for a two-bed), runs a scheme providing a number of apartments for short-term and overnight accommodation for residents' relatives and friends at economical rates. The space to the east of Great Arthur House, marked Central Piazza on Powell's competition plan, is bounded by the community building, a generous 22-by-15-by-4-metre (72-by-49-by-13-foot) room with a bar and stage used for parties, weekly chess tournaments, tenant meetings and bring-and-buy markets, above a more conspiratorial bar at lower-garden level.

The garden structure is naturally more public at street level and, through the use of the basement level of the pre-war buildings, more private at lower ground. To the east of the community building is a robust water and rose garden, while the ground-floor maisonettes have stepped access to the lower gardens. All the buildings have lock-up storage at basement level. The complex fragmentation leads naturally to a limit of deck lengths and therefore the self-policing of the close knowledge of neighbours rather than the one-liner and highly debatable continuous 'streets in the air' championed by Alison and Peter Smithson's competition entry for Golden Lane, which was then widely publicised in the press.

The graduation from the public bustle of Goswell Road to the reflective quiet of Golden Lane itself is carefully calibrated, as is that from the openness of the southern perimeter to the relatively closed northern edges of Baltic Street West and East. The architecture is, like the austerity-driven magic of Finnish post-war furniture and building design, simple and elegant. The warp buildings are all constructed of a brick and a half-thick sequence of dividing fin walls of five, six and seven storeys. These have subtle adjustments in line and contain the lightweight panels and aluminium window sections to the south. Brick turns to concrete in the tower topped by its distinctive roof garden and water tanks – like the hood of a windswept nun.

The weft buildings are on pilotis, and the staggered placing of the warp buildings opens up wonderful diagonal views like the pattern of a Mondrian risen from the pavement to form an integral part of urban design: intense simultaneous frames, views and colours – quite brilliant.

The contained architectural and urban control of the Golden Lane Estate becomes distinctly more problematic when seen as one of a complex series of urban territories that constitute its neighbourhood. The gleaming new estate stood in stark contrast to the adjacent buildings. To the south the patchwork of bombed-out sites running to St Paul's Cathedral and the river would form the most radical of London's post-war urban laboratories, creating London Wall, the Barbican Estate, Paternoster Square and the Museum of London. To the west across Aldersgate lies one of the 19th century's most ambitious and innovative infrastructure projects, the interchange at Smithfield, set cheek by jowl with the ancient foundation of St Bartholomew and one of the largest Carthusian monasteries in Europe, the Charterhouse, which tenaciously resists the surrounding urban onslaught and lies remarkably intact in confident quietude. To the east lies the earlier estate prototype of the 19th century, the Peabody, whose heavy 40-to-50-metre- (130-to-160-foot-) long blocks deny any communicative urban landscape between. They are set adjacent to the everyday bustle of the street market in Whitecross Street (see Chapter 4) and relieved by two green spaces: the little jewel of Fortune Park, named after the theatre built here in Elizabethan times; and the nonconformist burial ground of Bunhill Fields, resting place of, among others, Daniel Defoe, John Bunyan and William Blake. This territory once of outsiders continuing to Hoxton, now finds itself at the epicentre of the digital and so-called high-tech start-ups that have followed its cultural rise, born out of the influx of the arts community in the 1990s and its proximity to the financial pulse of the City.

The next chapter in this collage of ambitious urban experiments is underway with the construction of the Crossrail project which, at its interchange at Farringdon, will create a new focus of the scale of one of London's 19th-century hubs – London Bridge, King's Cross, Waterloo – each of which draws in excess of 30 million people annually into its hinterland.

Parish

Within the European city, the political boundaries defining the equivalent of the parish mark the community subset of the city beyond street or estate, but that lies within the next scale of political and social organisation – the borough, complete with town hall and local jurisdiction. Within London's Westminster, itself a city of a scale the equivalent of a modern German city, the Parish of St Martin-in-the-Fields developed between the conflicting powers of the people and the state.

Standing on a rise less than 2 kilometres (about a mile) west along the curving back of the north bank of the Thames from Ludgate, the western gateway of the Roman city of Londinium, the site on which the Parish Church of St Martin-in-the-Fields lies, has been used as a sacred place from at least AD 410, the year the Roman legions left Britain. During an archaeological dig as part of the renewal project (Eric Parry Architects, 2008), dramatic evidence was unearthed in the one small area undisturbed by preceding building campaigns, of a Roman-period sarcophagus and a number of other burials, eight of which were from the Anglo-Saxon period. From stratigraphic evidence it seems that the Anglo-Saxons left the well-built ruins of the Roman city to the east to decay, preferring the westward bank of the Thames to build their town along the route we know as the Strand – clearly derived from the German *Strand* (literally 'beach'), Frisian *strond*, Old English *strand*, Old Norse *strönd*. The earliest written evidence of a church on the site is from the 12th century. St Martin-in-the-Fields is one of several dedications in London to the 4th-century Bishop of Tours in France – whose famed act of charity, splitting his Roman legionary's cape to offer to a freezing beggar at the gates of the city of Amiens, reinforced these churches' philanthropic credentials. St Martin's came to prominence in the 16th century as favoured by King Henry VIII and his court, who created the parish boundary, some have observed cynically, to deal with plague victims at a safe distance from the Tudor palace of Westminster.[10] By the 18th century, the church was undersized for the growing parish, and its nave on the verge of collapse. Coincidentally, the rural setting 'in the fields' had been lost to development around the culturally fecund urban artery of St Martin's Lane, terminating then at Charing Cross to the south, and Seven Dials and High Holborn to the north. During the 17th and 18th centuries, the territory through which St Martin's Lane passed housed a galaxy of talent, marking the line between the court, the burgeoning estates and the relatively autonomous warren of Soho's streets and alleys, many of which in testament to their independence remain intact today. More than a physical confluence, it was also a cultural one, welcoming continental émigrés in search of a more liberal political climate. The gathering places were critical, given an absence of state patronage. Slaughters' Coffee House, first at numbers 74 and 75 and later at 82 St Martin's Lane, was a meeting place for the St Martin's Lane Academy initiated by the artist William Hogarth in 1735 as a continuation of his father-in-law James Thornhill's drawing school (1716–22) in Covent Garden, which itself followed Godfrey Kneller's academy (1711–16) in Great Queen Street, all more or less within a ten-minute walk of each other. The Theatre Royal, Drury Lane, to the east and the Haymarket theatre to the west, both fed on the public appetite for comment and satire, set between the Aldermen of the City and court and parliament of Westminster. The dramatist Henry Fielding, arguably the first great instigator of the modern novel, also became London's chief magistrate, founding the Bow Street Runners, considered London's first professional police force. George Frideric Handel – whose arrival in London in 1712 heralded fifty years of musical and operatic fervour, for nearly thirty of which it centred on the Theatre Royal Covent Garden – had friends in common with William Hogarth and in particular Thomas Coram, founder of the Foundling Hospital and the subject of one of Hogarth's finest portraits, to whose hospital Handel gave his manuscript copy of the *Messiah* (1741). Add to this the cabinetmakers' workshops of St Martin's Lane, foremost of which was Thomas Chippendale's for 28 years, and a picture begins to form of the social condition in which James Gibbs (1682–1754) was to create his parish church between 1721 and 1726.

Gibbs was chosen by recommendation and reputation; he had trained under Carlo Fontana in Rome, having received a Jesuit education. It is fascinating to realise that his six years in Rome were spent just three decades after the great trio of Francesco Borromini, Gian Lorenzo Bernini and Pietro da Cortona had left their indelible and brilliant architectural stamp on the city;

James Gibbs, St Martin-in-the-Fields, Westminster, London, 1726: view from New Zealand House, across Trafalgar Square
To the east, St Martin-in-the-Fields offers mediation and sanctuary in an avaricious world. To the north, the royal stables have become public museums; across the square the buildings of colonial and post-colonial diplomacy frame the stage of the national voice, leading south to the river and the seat of government.

and yet, as his own oeuvre suggests, he must also have been keenly aware of the early Christian churches: his circular unbuilt scheme for St Martin-in-the-Fields bears a striking resemblance to the plan of the Pantheon in Rome (1st century BC).

With his circular scheme deemed too large for the site and too expensive, Gibbs was sent back to the drawing board by the Parish and returned with the plan of the church transformed into an axial and more conventional nave with aisles. Maintained between the first and second iteration was the unorthodox juxtaposition of a classical portico facing St Martin's Lane pierced by the base of the spire. The mighty stone carapace is given weight by the four corner aedicules. Gibbs's model, currently loaned by the Parish to the Victoria and Albert Museum where it forms a key exhibit in the Architecture Gallery, is both an eloquent illustration of his precise architectural, spatial and construction intentions, but also a test of ideas – witness the different articulation of the hall on the north and south aspects of the model. It brings alive the debate that must have ensued in the Vestry or Parish rooms of the old church as the committee debated the propositions put forward by Gibbs. The ambition is palpable, remembering how this monumental white Portland stone building with its large grey lead roof would dwarf the surrounding essentially medieval buildings, all

James Gibbs, St Martin-in-the-Fields, Westminster, London, 1726: view of the Church Passage after renewal
The view westwards along the reconfigured church path shows the balustrade to the subterranean cloister, around which the spatial complex of an urban parish are drawn together.

at that time roofed in dirty warm-red terracotta tiles, and hemmed in by the terraces of the Royal Mews to the west. We know that the ambition was very much supported through, for instance, the vicar Zachariah Pearce's interpretation of the appropriate architecture for a Christian temple preserved in his sermon of dedication of 1724.

The evidence for the hemming in is clear from John Rocque's plan of Westminster (1746), among others, but also through the topographical sketches of the prolific George Scharf, drawn prior to the next urban transformation wrought by John Nash (1752–1835) between 1809 and 1826, in the creation of what was to become Trafalgar Square.

Nash, whose urban scenographic architecture owes a fair amount to his early practice of landscape architecture with Humphry Repton, understood how finely Gibbs's church, with its inflection, would read as his grand route south to Carlton House passed across Pall Mall and offered views into the new public space to the east, which in Nash's mind was to be the meeting point of his two envisaged axes – the first running south from Regent's Park to Carlton House and St James's Park, and the other due north along St Martin's Lane from the new space leading south to Whitehall, creating a street from Charing Cross to Bloomsbury to reveal Robert Smirke's British Museum (1846) in a new square. At the same time, the great church of St George's Bloomsbury (1730) by Nicholas Hawksmoor was, like St Martin's, enmeshed in the swooning tight urban grain. The carving up of London's political landscape by Nash, Smirke and Sir John Soane reflects their patronages and was put boldly in a letter from Nash to Soane in 1822: 'it occurred to me that our appointments are perfectly constitutional, I the King, You the Lords, and Your friend Smirke, the Commons, and the blood instantly rushed to my face seeing, or fancying, that you wanted to dethrone me.'[11]

While Nash's plan for a new street from Charing Cross to Bloomsbury was not executed, his transformation of the area surrounding St Martin-in-the-Fields was. To understand its ambitious nature it is worth studying the plan which, by redefining the St Martin's workhouse and removing the Royal Mews – essentially stabling for the palace – to the north, created a frontage to the new public space with natural gardens, painting and sculpture. Cockspur Street was enlarged to the southwest, and Pall Mall to the east devised as a grand vista with a monumental building between to house the Royal College of Physicians and the Union Club.

James Gibbs, St Martin-in-the-Fields, Westminster, London, 1726: diagonal view of the interior
The body of James Gibbs's church, representative of the Parish, completed in 1726, reset by John Nash with a north range of buildings that included a school and burial vaults. Re-ordered in 2006–8 with the school and full basement as a centre for the homeless – the Connection at St Martin's – together with a new subterranean hall, music rehearsal facilities, the expansion of exhibition and restaurant space. This complex set of spaces forms a crucial spiritual and humanitarian quarter on Trafalgar Square, itself London's principal public space.

The great space that we know as Trafalgar Square was bisected by a proposal for a freestanding classical temple, intended to house the Royal Academy of Arts and discreetly separating equestrian statues of George III to the west and George IV to the east, who were famously at odds with each other. These would have formed centrepieces to two squares, each in view of Hubert Le Sueur's equestrian statue of Charles I (1633) standing at the confluence of Cockspur Street, the Strand and Charing Cross. To the south of the church, Nash envisaged a triangular site formed by the Strand and what is now Duncannon Street, thus exposing the southern flank of the church.

This building is now South Africa House, but was initially envisaged to house the Vicarage, the Athenaeum Club and the Golden Cross Hotel. The urban isolation of Gibbs's masterpiece was established by an open rectangular churchyard formed over brick burial vaults that constituted a level stylobate against the fall of the land southwards to the river. The walls of this new base were articulated by heavy vermiculation, as if unearthed, and were topped by iron railings copied from Gibbs's originals around the portico. To the east of the church's new-found urban space were a series of large parcels to let, later to be formed into Nash's triangular block with its four 'pepper pot' corner cupolas, through which ran the Lowther Arcade that once specialised in children's toys before being consumed by Coutts Bank. To the north of the churchyard, Nash proposed a block incorporating a 'police office'; a central plot to be exchanged for other properties to be demolished; a terrace facing the church acquired by the Parish and developed by Nash as a vicarage; a building housing the vestry incorporating older joinery to a fine parish room set over a mortuary room leading to the burial vaults below; and a school, on ground given by King George IV, children from which used the churchyard to play in.

This 'perfectly constitutional'[12] vision for a royal forum as London's first 'public' space has a set piece that cleansed the crusty Hogarthian hinterland of workhouses, pillories and freak shows and established the formal outlines of Trafalgar Square. The complex ebb and flow of the citizens' voice and that of the authorities echo the acceptance of its presence and its potential as a place of demonstration and often angry expression in which St Martin-in-the-Fields has often found a pivotal mediating role. The church is a pillar of the establishment, being the parish church to both Buckingham Palace and Downing Street. It is as well the Admiralty church and boasts a royal balcony pew and its facing equivalent for the Admiralty, both overlooking the sanctuary. The other side of the establishment coin is the independence of its vicars' voices, beginning most forcefully with the Reverend Dick Sheppard, who was appointed in 1914, became the Honorary Chaplain to the King, and served at the battlefront in the First World War, returning to open the crypt as a refuge and night shelter to both the homeless and particularly the psychologically traumatised soldiery passing to and from France through Charing Cross station. Sheppard subsequently became an ardent pacifist and, on retiring from St Martin's, became the Dean of Canterbury Cathedral where his tomb lies in the cloister, and is still a place of annual pilgrimage by members of the congregation and The Connection at St Martin's – a powerful voice in both the national and local support of the homeless today. With its close adjacency to South Africa House, the church also found itself at the centre of the anti-Apartheid movement and is held in high regard for its support of that cause by many people, including Archbishop Desmond Tutu, who feels a close bond of trust and friendship as a result. It is said that the idea of both the human rights organisation Amnesty International and the homelessness charity Shelter germinated through the church and its activities, and it became an important meeting place for those opposing the Greater London Council's crass plans for the obliteration of Covent Garden in the 1970s, with the support of the Vicar Austen Williams. Called the 'church of the ever-open door' by Dick Sheppard (a description which has stuck), Nash's burial vaults designed for the dead became a densely used labyrinth of spaces for the living – the musicians, the large Chinese community, the kitchens and their staff, concert-goers, the homeless and their needs for laundry washing, feeding and medical care. On the extensive site designed by Gibbs and Nash at the heart of Westminster and London, all the constituent parts of contemporary London society mix with the common spirit of generosity and relative even-handedness.

In his apocalyptic vision in *Nineteen Eighty-Four* (1949), George Orwell set the ultimate inversion of the powerful evil of authoritarianism as the metamorphosis of St Martin's from a place of care to the nightmare of 'a museum used for propaganda displays of various kinds – scale models of rocket bombs and Floating Fortresses, waxwork tableaux illustrating enemy atrocities and the like.'[13]

Nash's vaults did not work: the lead-lined coffins leaked, the stone shelves filled up quickly and created an expensive maintenance problem for the Parish, and within forty years they were defunct. By 1995, with the arrival of Nicholas Holtam as Vicar, the fabric was in a miserable state and, subsequent to one of the regular memorial services, a group emerged to set about a renewal project initiated by an architectural competition which was won by Eric Parry Architects in 2001 after a lengthy process.

At the same time, the reordering of the square by Foster + Partners – which was to win the World Squares for All prize from RIBA/English Heritage – introduced a pedestrianised promenade under the steps of the National Gallery that, while ridding the square of traffic, reinforced the spectacle of the bear pit containing Sir Edwin Lutyens's fountains (1939) and Sir Edwin Landseer's lions (1867). The so-called square has always been a frustrating place in urban terms, neither fish nor foul, and has been the setting for heroically ironic architectural projects, including Ben Nicholson's 'Travulgar Square Scheme' – produced under the tutelage of Daniel Libeskind and Alberto Pérez-Gómez at the Architectural Association in 1976–7 – which, with its giant consuming pigeon, echoes the fantastical drawings of Jean-Jacques Lequeu (1757–1826).

The style wars of Prince Charles, with his attack on Ahrends, Burton and Koralek's National Gallery competition-winning proposal for an extension of 1985 – 'a monstruous carbuncle on the face of a much-loved and elegant friend'[14] – and the rejection of Zaha Hadid's radical, or Allies and Morrison's polite, proposals for the redevelopment of Northumberland House in the competition of 1986, led to the feeble historicist masks that were built. The question of simultaneity at an urban scale is however thrown into focus in the debate of the origins and development of the square through the historical layers that make up its rich hinterland. The project for the renewal of the site and church of St Martin-in-the-Fields provides an example of the power of social adjacency and spatial simultaneity.

At street level it involves the reordering of the scale of enclosures to increase the church path lying between Nash's north range of buildings and Gibbs's church. The clarification of entrances to the vicarage, the Parish offices, the homeless refuge, the new subterranean spaces and reinforcing the sacred passage from the shadow of the west to the luminosity of the east was a primary goal of the project. In the enlarged church path at the west end, but placed a little behind the line of the portico, a new glass-walled pavilion makes an accessible entrance to the subterranean level of the 18th-century crypt. The equivalent plan form of the pavilion is reversed into the ground, eastwards but on the same axis, to form an open cloister and lightwell two storeys below, around which are congregated three new important double-height spaces: a chapel that terminates the axis, a church hall to the west and a music rehearsal space. This part of the project includes rooms for associated groups like the strong Chinese community affiliated with St Martin-in-the-Fields and the centre for the homeless that occupies the lower-ground level of Nash's terrace and the entire body of the old school at the east end of the terrace. The Parish has its centre in the vestry, and to the west on St Martin's Place the vicar and assistant vicars live on its several levels. The church, restored and with a reconfigured east end, holds 27 services a week, is a constant venue for concerts and recitals and has an enormous outreach. Together these interconnected spaces create, with an ever open door, a place of refuge and contemplation, but also with the crypt a busy restaurant and café whose profits support the Parish and create a meeting place adjacent to the politics of engagement of Trafalgar Square, Westminster and London.

In concluding this chapter we hope that it is clear that simultaneity is pertinent at all scales of making, from a room to a city, and that the reverberations from one to the other underpin the potential potency of their interrelations. Simultaneity implies a thinking beyond physical boundaries and transparencies to the social adjacencies of accumulated spatial arrangements and their narrative and choreography. The notion of typical situation is equally relevant to our next chapter concerning streets.

References

1. Dalibor Vesely, *Architecture in the Age of Divided Representation*, The MIT Press (Cambridge, MA), 2004, p 303.
2. Georges Perec, *Species of Spaces and Other Pieces* [*Espèces d'espaces*, 1974, etc], translated by John Sturrock, Penguin (London), 1997.
3. Edmund Engelman, *Berggasse 19: Sigmund Freud's Home and Offices, Vienna 1938*, University of Chicago Press (Chicago and London), 1981, passim.
4. Ernest Jones, 'The Medical Student (1873–1881)', in Ernest Jones, *The Life and Work of Sigmund Freud*, Plunkett Lake Press (Lexington, MA), 2014, book I, chapter 4, Kindle edition.
5. Ernest Jones, 'Introduction', in *ibid*.
6. Quoted in Marcus Binney, *Country Life Annual*, 1970, p 130.
7. Ian Nairn, *Nairn's London* [1966], revised edition, Penguin (London), 1988, p 24.
8. 'Chamberlin, Powell and Bon' in Muriel Emanuel (ed.), *Contemporary Architects*, Macmillian (London), 1980, pp 233–5.
9. 'Men of the Year 1952', *Architects' Journal*, vol 177, no 3020, 15 January 1953, p 72.
10. John McMaster, *A Short History of the Royal Parish of St Martin-in-the-Fields, London, WC*, G Holder & Sons (London), 1916, p 14.
11. Quoted in John Summerson, *John Nash: Architect to King George IV*, George Allen & Unwin (London), 1949, p 257.
12. *Ibid*.
13. Quoted in Nicholas Holtam, *A Room with a View*, SPCK (London), 2000, p xiii.
14. A speech by HRH The Prince of Wales at the 150th anniversary of the Royal Institute of British Architects (RIBA), Royal Gala Evening at Hampton Court Palace, 30 May 1984 (witnessed by the author), http://www.princeofwales.gov.uk/media/speeches/speech-hrh-the-prince-of-wales-the-150th-anniversary-of-the-royal-institute-of (accessed 5 December 2014).

4 Kinetics

Whitecross Street has long been part of the connective tissue between the City of London and its adjacent boroughs. Remembered as a thriving London street market in the early part of the 20th century, the connection was severed by the building of the Barbican Estate in the 1960s and 1970s, after which the market continued residually. With the growth of the northern city fringe and the creation of a cultural centre in the bombed-out shell of St Luke's Old Street (built in 1733 to designs by Nicholas Hawksmoor and John James), the latent demand was there, but it took a light-handed infrastructure project by Islington Borough Council and the architectural and landscape practice muf, involving street resurfacing and the delivery of power and water to the assigned portions of market stalls, for it to blossom spectacularly.

Whitecross Street, London, typical life of the street on a working day, 2014.
Whitecross Street looking south towards the City at midday, to the left the gabled ends of the five-storey Peabody Estate, to the right typical three-storey London terraces, the intensity of the market in full swing.

While the street market principally feeds a lunchtime clientele of office workers from the fast-growing Clerkenwell and Old Street territories, it has as a long-standing neighbour a city parade of shops in the undercroft of a 1970s local authority housing scheme, adding to the legacy of 19th-century Peabody Trust housing and warehouses behind the nonconformist burial ground of Bunhill Fields. The whole makes a very positive and lively diurnal street use pattern – although it remains undistinguished in comparison to the monuments of the church and the Barbican, and a lengthy section comprising one flank of the Peabody Estate creates an awkward barrier of raised ground-floor residential use. As an experience it compresses to almost single file at its busiest periods of food selling, with its accompanying sensory intensity; and then the pavements expand with the retreat of the market stalls to accommodate the external tables of cafés, bars and restaurants.

Whitecross Street, London, typical life of the street on a working day, 2014
A little further north at 6.30 a.m., café tables occupy the widened pavements before the market stalls arrive.

The reasons for highlighting the Whitecross Street condition are manifold. Firstly, in a scruffy London way, it illustrates a medium or midpoint between the numbing onslaught of the out-of-town shopping mall surrounded by a sea of asphalt car parks that sets human proximity at the scale of the parking grid and the shopping trolley, and the articulation of the street in the super-dense condition of cities such as Mumbai (see the following section), where the thinness of a garment separates passers-by. Secondly, it draws to attention a key concern of this chapter, which is the kinetic experience of the street as a contribution to the urban condition. Thirdly, with pertinence to the subject of context, it aids an analysis of what it is that creates the typicality of a place that we can ascribe, say, to the Parisian street, Rome's historic Borgo district, the New York grid or the London village. Fourthly, it attests to the fact that all these places are the result of wilful decisions – urban, political, economic, design and above all social – and that the layers of these, representing both radical and small adjustments, in large part answer the question of typicality and context at closer reading.

Bhuleshwar, Mumbai

Martin Charles's photographs of Bhuleshwar Road in Mumbai, now more than 25 years old, capture a complex static architectural setting and the rapid flow of a bustling street. A brilliant photographer of architecture, Charles was using a camera with 5-by-4-inch (13-by-10-centimetre) film, poised on a tripod with a horizon line pitched above the heads of the crowd, as he himself perched on a wooden crate. It would take him a little less than a half hour to set up, refer to complex notes of previous shoots, check his composition and dismantle his kit. The sea of benignly intrigued staring faces bears witness to the strangeness of the event, but behind the momentary stillness can be observed the continuous mercantile flow, slightly blurred, crossing the axis of the architectural frame. Behind this movement are the openings to the shops announced by their accompanying signboards, and

Bhuleshwar Road, Mumbai, photographed in 1986
Reflecting urban layering, Martin Charles's photograph shows onlookers in the foreground, the flow of the street behind and number 148 straight ahead. The waiters look from their living quarters on the first-floor restaurant balcony.

above the evidence of dense inhabitation, sacred and secular jostling the skyline – a frozen reflection of the scene below.

The district of Bhuleshwar has developed in parallel with the modern history of Mumbai (formerly Bombay). Control of the Portuguese settlement passed to the English in 1661 as a result of the marriage contract between Charles II and Catherine of Portugal. Subsequently the East India Company established its headquarters in Bombay Castle with its walled fort. As Bombay developed, the form remained separated from the growing mercantile structure to the north by a green swathe known as the Esplanade, to be used as a killing field in times of conflict but otherwise as a strolling space between colonisers and colonised on which the power of restraint and coded manners of dress were exhibited through the ritualised battle of such games as cricket and polo. The walls of the fort were demolished in the 1860s, and the seven islands of the peninsula, once separated by sea and swamp, were rapidly filled to create the single landmass of the city today.

In 1907 Bhuleshwar was described in the *Bombay Gazetteer* as 'at the heart of the busiest portion of the city',[1] and a 1901 census gave the density for the district as 399 persons per acre (986 per hectare).[2] Over the years, along a clearly low-rise urban setting when compared to cities like Hong Kong, the natural growth of population has dramatically intensified Bhuleshwar's urban density and given way to ordinary forms of life and conditions perhaps without precedent in the history of cities.

The ordering of the urban framework that allows this kind of density to function, as it has loosely for more than 150 years, with an intensity of use that has continually been ratcheted up to today's level, is the basis of the following analysis which is partial but quite typical of the contemporary Indian city and with distinct similarities to the urban condition of cities of the Levant, Iran and Pakistan – in essence wonderfully rich, directly participatory and shared space, in stark contrast to the battery-fed, fast-food homogeneity of shopping experience in the average westernised city, as eloquently summarised by Gillian Tindall in her biography of Bombay, *City of Gold* (1982):

> Today it is, like all Indian cities, in Western eyes, ramshackle, disorganised, apparently in need of urgent social first aid. Yet in comparison with Bombay, many more illustrious western national or federal capitals seem like small

towns expressed in a grandiose manner – self-regarding, provincial, fossilised in one particular period or rôle; and others seem to have passed their prime and are losing their *raison d'être*, like old hedgerows growing out, hollowing at the centre. But Bombay lives.[3]

At the heart of Bhuleshwar lies Bhuleshwar Road, and at street level the whole district – with the exception of explicitly sacred territories, which includes the streets during the frequent religious festivals – acts as a marketplace. The less accessible interiors of the dense buildings are used as godowns (warehousing), while the most valuable commercial spaces are unsurprisingly those at ground floor with street frontages. The larger urban territories mark the continuing complex balance between the sacred and the

Eric Parry Architects, survey plan of 148 Bhuleshwar Road, Mumbai, 2014 (from 1985–6 survey)
The ground-floor site plan shows the location of the buildings surveyed in detail.

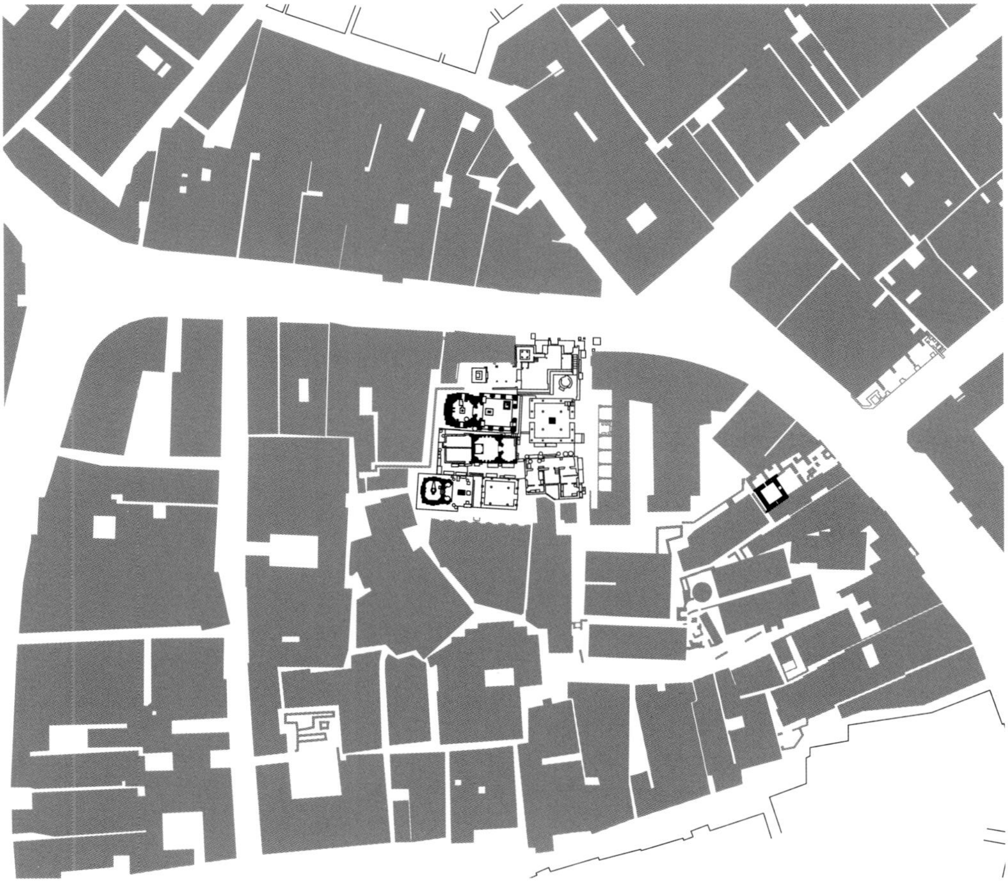

secular: the Mahadevi temple complex which once stood beside a stepped tank (one of seven in Bombay with histories stretching back over a thousand years, the last remaining example being that at Banganga whose structure is briefly mentioned in Chapter 1), and the market, the formal enclosing building of which is at the head of the middle of three market streets (the Bhoiwada Lanes), laid out perpendicularly to the central ovular-shaped Bhuleshwar urban core around which the later city streets were developed.

Suketu Mehta, whose book *Maximum City: Bombay Lost and Found* (2005) digs much deeper than the statisticians' facts, vividly describes the impulses that draw incomers to Mumbai from the relative tranquillity of rural life.[4] The assault on personal space, the continuous noise, the pollutants and the discomforts are an investment for future personal and familial progress. There is a superficial answer to the physical corollary in the morphology of the urban grain, in figure-ground diagrams, which indicate the close-knit intricacy of the Mumbai grain relative to other cities. The real answer, and an important one for the future of the more urbanised planet, lies in the architectural framework and a closer observation of the diurnal patterns of use it harbours.

Commonly a building with an average frontage of perhaps 6 metres (20 feet) will house two complete shops with a dividing corridor, leading to the upper floors, the first of which will be for commercial use with dwellings above. The depths of these highly prized crustaceous units will only be 450 millimetres (17¾ inches) while locked. The units during business hours reveal carefully composed displays.

Beyond the shelter of the building and the narrow pavement width, barrow space is rented on the main street, a single pitch being used by several barrow owners in a day. The small side streets such as Bhoiwadi 3rd Lane are bazaars, sometimes covered, each like the alleys in a supermarket, dealing with a particular and related world of goods. While the Western vision of a supermarket is a shed in a desert of tarmac, the dense fabric of Bhuleshwar acts as a backdrop and route for an abundance of religious festival parades that culminate in the many temple complexes in this part of the city. The streets are shared by gods and people, and it is this that allows personal identity and order to exist within the dense and apparently chaotic fabric.

Number 148 Bhuleshwar Road is not a particularly distinguished building, but it does have a typical 19th-century balconied facade which masks a rich and varied use. The ground floor is occupied by a tobacconist and a dried fruit

Shopfronts on Bhuleshwar Road, Mumbai, photographed in 1986
In this photographic print by the late photographer Martin Charles, one is immersed in the density of the human and situational context of Bhuleshwar, Mumbai. The onlookers speak of the life of the dense frontages in the background.

merchant, while one of the walls of the corridor leading to the shrine at the rear of the building becomes by day the shop of a seller of nuts and dried fruit. The owner of the shop also owns the godown, a storage room at the rear. On the floor at the rear of the corridor next to the *mandapa* (pillared pavilion) of the shrine, nuts are split with expert precision on a large manual guillotine, then weighed for immediate sale, or stored in the airtight glass jars that line the walls. The shrine at the rear of this building, dedicated to Vishnu and Rakhmani, is a domed structure of an earlier date than the rest of the building. When these gods are awake, a neon light illuminates the staring figures and the mythic landscape of the marble steps to the shrine. The stairs lead to the lobby of the thali vegetarian restaurant where the owner sits, master of the cash drawer, under an image of Ganesh – the god of wellbeing, protector of wealth and a symbol of modern Bombay. Fourteen boys, three cooks and a supervisor work and sleep on this floor of the building. The daily routine is gruelling, with shifts between the purchase, preparation, cooking and serving of food occupying 18 hours. The second-floor front room is a dormitory rented by a village to house its menfolk working in Bombay. The third floor is a family dwelling by night and an office for Rajasthani textile and jewellery merchants by day.

The building is a rented property and, like much of Bombay's fabric, stands by virtue of the developmental inertia caused by the fixed rent act. As we surveyed the building in 1986,[5] the wealthy tenants of the third floor were having their rooms redecorated, and in the process had the stucco surrounds to the balcony openings removed. With increasing regularity, when the

Eric Parry, sketches of 148 Bhuleshwar Road, Mumbai, 1986
The first shows chapatti making in a first-floor restaurant kitchen; the second, a third-floor apartment.

scaffolding is dismantled after building renovations, the characteristic teak balconies have been demolished or replaced with no regard to detail.

Rockefeller Center, New York

At first it may seem an odd juxtaposition, but the cities of Mumbai and New York – the latter with reference to Manhattan – share some obvious parallels. Both are peninsulas: Mumbai, 23 kilometres (14 miles) long by an average of

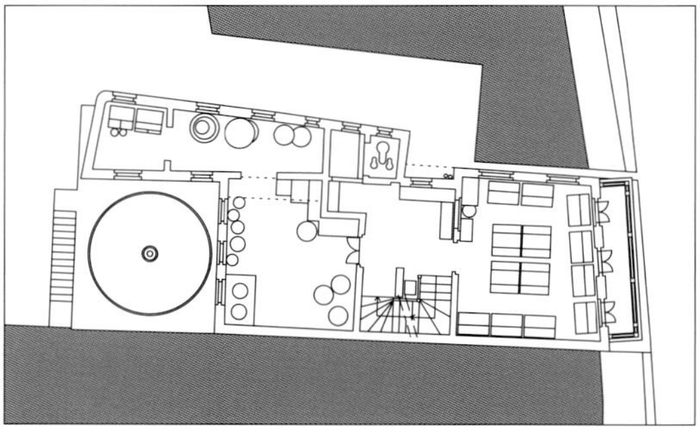

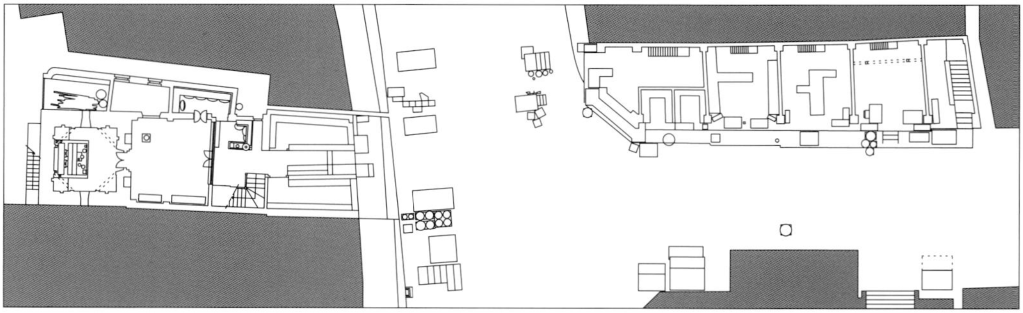

Eric Parry Architects, ground-floor plan of shops, godown and shrine at 148 Bhuleshwar Road, Mumbai, 2014 (from 1985–6 survey)
Both of these plans illustrate the human and elaborate interiors of the shops, godown and shrine that punctuate 148 Bhuleshwar Road, one among many that amount to the prolixity of contemporary Mumbai.

5 kilometres (3 miles) wide, is the result of a string of islands that still mark the high ground of the city, which then developed through the land fill of the swampy ground between them into a single entity; and Manhattan, the same length and a more regular width, is a rocky outcrop set between the Hudson River and the East River. Both developed from colonial settlements at the tip of their respective peninsulas – the Dutch and then the English in New York, the Portuguese and the English in Bombay. The Dutch fought and subjugated the indigenous American tribes, while the British separated themselves, administered and traded for gain in Bombay. In the early 19th century Bombay was a walled town, with a compact harbour and esplanade separating this southern colonial and military settlement from the native town to the north, beyond which were sparse suburbs set in coconut groves with clustered settlements on the coast and rice paddies inland. The mid-19th century brought the first cotton mills and railway lines, together with extensive new docks. The American Civil War created five phenomenal boom years when cotton from India via Bombay was the staple of English mills, followed by a painful retrenching, but growth continued. Apart from the infrastructure of industry, the grand colonial administrative buildings and the

financial powerhouses, the city was a labyrinthine mass of close-knit buildings on the flats that now were the real heart of the city. Ownership is and has been split into ever diminishing sections of land, which in large part accounts for the typically close urban grain mentioned earlier. Only at the beginning of the 20th century did the authorities, in the form of an Improvement Trust, impose a degree of order by creating some new roads and widening others, evident in the infrequency of roads in the map of Mumbai.

In contrast to the vigorous, haphazard and episodic growth of Mumbai, New York's grid was established by a Commissioners' Plan for Manhattan in 1811. The Commission was made up of just three men. In charge was Robert Morris, one of the Founding Fathers of the United States. They engaged the surveyor John Randel Jr to map Manhattan, and on the basis of this a uniform grid of 12 avenues, each 100 feet (30 metres) wide, and 155 cross streets, each 50 feet (15 metres) wide, was imposed, leaving intact the old southerly grids of Greenwich Village, the Stuyvesant Estate and the Bloomingdale Road, an ancient track which was to be renamed Broadway and which at critical points for the new grid lay obliquely.

The grid follows the precedent of other cities, notably Philadelphia, whose 100-by-150-yard (91-by-137-metre) grid had been established by William Penn and his surveyor Thomas Holme in the 1680s. The planned city was bounded by two rivers, like New York spaced approximately two miles (three kilometres) apart, and ordered around its one central and four outlying squares, forming a central rectangle of 1,850 yards by 1,050 yards (1,690 by 960 metres) – a yard being the average of a stride. New York was emulating Philadelphia, the first capital of the United States between 1790 and 1800. The political rhetoric that underpinned the form of these city grids was that of equating the burgeoning new world with the ancient Roman republic in the pragmatism of its cities, roads and the continent-wide approach to industry.

The resultant New York grid with its epic scale, essentially running from 13th Street to 130th Street, is characterised by the major north–south corridors of the avenues crossed by the smaller dimension of the east–west streets which, like the weft of a textile, constantly connect the shores of the two rivers. By the mid-19th century, with the grid filling, the need for public space for 'walking and driving' was becoming urgent and the idea of a central park for Manhattan was gathering momentum, formalised through debate and publications. In 1863 this resulted in the territory between 59th and 110th Streets and Fifth and Eighth Avenues, later called Central Park West, being adopted and cleared in one of the most visionary, democratic and philanthropic conceptions of modern urban planning. Given the commercial frenzy that gripped New York at the time, it was an inspired moment to offer an extraordinary balance to the future of the city. It became the magnet that drew development northwards, and in turn was the catalyst for the later development of the Rockefeller Center (discussed below).

The conditions and pressures that led directly to the 1916 New York Zoning ordinance (which created a shoulder to the height of the street) were the advent of the steel frame and the elevator, which had released buildings in a vertical dimension and had done so particularly in the Wall Street banking district, creating dim canyons out of the pre-existing street plan. The ordinance had two principal rulings. The first was sectional, creating a notional line from the centre of the street inclining to allow a minimum angle of light. The building frontage of a plot could rise vertically until it intersected this line, above which any additional storeys had to be set back in order not to breach it. The second rule was planimetric, created in

51st Street, New York, crossing Manhattan east–west
51st Street and Fifth Avenue looking north to the Italian apex of the topographic rising of this section of the city.

Raymond Hood, Rockefeller Center, New York, 1939: raised diagonal view across Rockefeller Plaza
Looking southwest from the roof garden of the Italian pavilion over the Plaza to the NBC News Room, and beyond it Christie's New York exhibition and auction rooms.

order to set back walls from boundaries which would create court spaces with windows; however, when the plan area had been reduced to 25 per cent of the site area, then its vertical dimension became, in theory, infinite. The decade between 1916 and 1926 saw the architectural response in a series of landmark buildings and, with them, the growth of a number of prominent architectural practices paralleling the burgeoning contracting companies and the rise of a relatively new figure, the specialist construction manager, as the separation into two parts of the publication of the Rockefeller City by the Architectural Forum in January 1932 bears witness.[6] The first part was devoted to the architectural design, the second to engineering and business. The second part opens under the title of 'Organisation for Cooperation' with a diagram, by now very familiar to practitioners, with management at the centre separating the meddling hands of designer and owner. New York's nomadic heart found its most socially articulate form in the Rockefeller Center which was completed, ceremonially at least, with the fastening of the last rivet in November 1939. The constraints and opportunities that created the Rockefellers' buildings are intrinsically bound to the physical development of the city and to the ambitions and fortunes of its citizens.

Raymond Hood, Rockefeller Center, New York: drawing published on the cover of the *Architectural Forum*, vol 56, no 1, 1932
The emblematic image was published on the cover of an edition of the *Architectural Forum* focusing on the architectural design; the sequel was a drawing of the steel frame under construction, with a focus on building technology and management.

Here I do not intend to concentrate on its overall and very impressive soaring forms and architectural antecedents (including precedents from European sources, such as Bruno Taut's *House of Heaven* project of 1920), which have been well defined in other publications, but rather to scrutinise more closely its effect at ground level. It merits close study because of its undoubted success and because it has been superficially emulated globally and remains an often quoted metropolitan precedent for urban designers. The three urban grid blocks that now make up the ground of the Rockefeller Center are each 312 by 80 metres (1,023 by 262 feet) and were conveyed as a lot to Columbia College in 1814 by the State of New York, who in turn had purchased the land as an established botanical and apothecary garden. They were bounded to the south consecutively by West 48th, 49th and 50th Streets; to the west by Sixth Avenue with at the time the elevated tramway at its centre; and to the east by Fifth Avenue. The estate had been under serious consideration by the agents of the Metropolitan Opera for its urban rehousing. Given a free hand it is clear, as some of the early brainstorming schemes show, that the scheme's principal architect Raymond Hood (1881–1934) and others dreamed of creating a Babylonian-scale megastructure with diagonally structured arcades converging at the central ordinance-conforming eruption and reminiscent of most of Hood's work. This public space was first proposed for the site in 1928 by the Metropolitan Opera Company's architect Benjamin Wistar Morris and was entirely focused on a monumental setting for the proposed opera house. It was raised above street level and set between three commercial buildings looking like a set of cenotaphs, each pierced by grand arcades leading to a continuous colonnade that girdled the space. Luckily

Raymond Hood, Rockefeller Center, New York, 1939
The entrance of the Radio City Music Hall at the corner of the Avenue of the Americas and 50th Street. The auditorium, seating 6,000, presses to the edges of the block's width, defining the breadth of the stage and the length of the iconic chorus line of the Rockettes.

for the city, under the pragmatic watch of John D Rockefeller Jr, the builder and managing agent John R Todd and his architects of choice Reinhard & Hofmeister rapidly established a preferred development plan called G-3 which broadly proved to be the diagrammatic form of the completed project. The proposals meant the demolition of 280 lots mostly containing brownstones – New York's tenement type – large numbers of which were thriving in use as brothels and speakeasies (where alcohol was consumed illicitly during the Prohibition). The project no doubt appealed to Rockefeller as a potentially lucrative investment at an epic scale, but there were at least three other aspects that were part of his agenda and all involved social and physical 'cleansing'. The first was social. He had led for several years the men's bible class in the Fifth Avenue Baptist Church, was a committed prohibitionist and had served as foreman to a grand jury for six months investigating organised prostitution. In purchasing the leases to enable the development, the Rockefeller Foundation paid dearly – so much so that the Metropolitan Opera company declined further involvement; and his determination to push ahead with the project at the time of the stock market crash on 29 October 1929 must have been fuelled by his puritan zeal. The second aspect was related to placemaking and his support for a group of particular projects in that regard, which included some twenty years of financial backing for the excavation of the *agora* in Athens, the building and endowment of the Palestine Archaeological Museum and, closer to home, the restoration of the historic centre of Williamsburg. They suggest a deep-rooted interest in the social and community use of space through history. Several aspects relate directly to the programme of use at the Center: the powerful populist voice of Radio City and his enthusiastic support for both it and the Plaza, unprecedented in New York real estate of the time.

The whole presaged the 1950s plan to create a grand site for music including the Metropolitan Opera that was to become the Lincoln Center and Plaza. Raised podia are generally the death knell of public space, as are undercrofts, appealing as they may be on the drawing board. This is clearly illustrated by this example of privilege and exclusivity – and it was equally true of the post-war Paternoster Square project in London to the north of St Paul's Cathedral, which, apart from the entrances to offices, boasted little more than a solitary newsagent and some public toilets, and through its raised level also served to diminish the Cathedral's presence. The positive aspect of the early proposal for the Rockefeller Center site was twofold. Most important was the public function, for while the opera exited the stage, the embryonic world-embracing technology of radio entered, with the dual aspect of the vast auditorium – Edward Durell Stone's Radio City Music Hall (1932) seating 6,000, and his 3,700-seat Center Theatre playing second fiddle to it – and up to 35 state-of-the-art studios for the National Broadcasting Corporation (NBC – originally established as the Radio Corporation of America in 1919 to combat British dominance of the communications world). The facilities, more advanced than any others and sumptuously fitted out from foyer to washrooms with contemporary finishes, artwork and furniture, together with the impresario genius of a team led by 'Roxy' (Samuel L Rothafel), drew

Raymond Hood, Rockefeller Center, New York, 1939: live broadcast outside NBC studios
At street level with one of the daily routine of news interviews underway.

continuous crowds both to the theatres and to the surrounding public spaces, the Plaza, at their head. The two worlds are bound by *Wisdom: A Voice from the Clouds* (1934), the limestone bas-relief sculpture by Lee Lawrie which hovers like Rockefeller's apotheosis above the quadruple-height central entrance, making it visible above Paul Manship's gilded bronze *Prometheus* (1934) plunging earthwards with the gift of fire in front of the fountain wall of the lower Plaza at concourse level. It is, along with the crafting that celebrates every other public threshold, great stagecraft, only occasionally rising to memorable art. The scale of the public art commissioning is extraordinary. Hartley Burr Alexander, Professor of Philosophy at the University of Southern California, was employed to develop a theme for the Center of which he wrote:

Raymond Hood, Rockefeller Center, New York, 1939: entrance to the Rainbow Room, the Observation Deck and the NBC studios
Looking eastwards along 49th Street, the entrance to the observation deck with its views across New York and down over the roof gardens of the Center.

> The theme should open out of the structure and uses of the city itself, and to this there are two angles: (1) as an architectural monument the [Rockefeller] City is unique, and as an architectural interpretation of the civilization will inevitably challenge comparison with the great monuments of other civilisations; (2) as a social enterprise of the greatest importance for the future of the culture not only of North America but in the world.[7]

An advisory art committee was formed in response and was made up from the most conservative minds of American art politics of the 1930s, the last decade before New York threw off Europe's art-world hegemony. Nelson Rockefeller, a collector of contemporary art, was, it seems, responsible for lifting the horizon of artists to an international level for the main lobby of the RCA Building (now the GE Building). Alfred Barr, the director of the Museum of Modern Art, which was at first housed in the Center before finding its permanent home, accurately called the list of artists that had been chosen by the committee 'competent mediocrity'.[8]

Raymond Hood, Rockefeller Center, New York, 1939: view of Lee Lawrie's *Wisdom: A Voice from the Clouds* (1934)
Lee Laurie's bas-relief sculpture leans heavily over the entrance to the quadruple-height interior mediated by the refractive cast glass screen.

The architect and construction manager were sent to lobby Europe to solicit interest in the ten 5-by-6-metre (17-by-20-foot) panels in the RCA Building and were met by reactions ranging from complete indifference from Picasso (if not his gallerists) to Diego Rivera being 'pleased' with his location at the front entrance and Josep Maria Sert and Frank Brangwyn's acceptance of working monochromatically. The destruction of Rivera's masterwork with its portrait of Lenin, titled *Man at the Crossroads Looking with Uncertainly but with Hope and High Vision to the Choosing of a Course Leading to a New and Better Future*, had a tragic inevitability given the titanic clash of political dogmas. The same was true of some excellent work by the Italian Attilio Piccirilli, whose cast glass panel *Advance Forever Eternal Youth, Art is Labor, Labor is Art* was removed from the Italian building in 1940. The three international buildings fronting onto Fifth Avenue – the British, the French and the Italian – were part of an explicit bid to raise the Center's credentials from city to state and beyond, but also created an identity to the passages of 49th and 50th Streets and particularly to the sloping ground, now fondly known as the Channel or La Manche, that runs between the British and French buildings and leads to the Plaza by a ceremonial stairway – reduced by the ramp to garden rather than building scale. The Plaza level is part of a spatial adventure that creates a public route under the entire central section of the whole, stretching back to Sixth Avenue. Connecting as it does to the New York Subway

Raymond Hood, Rockefeller Center, New York, 1939: view of Paul Manship's *Prometheus* (1934)
View looking north from 49th Street into the sunken plaza, with Paul Manship's gilded bronze sculpture centre stage, surrounded by the seasonal restaurant tables.

system and to the Radio City complex, it acts as a busy lower-ground interchange which in turn has the benefit of feeding the retail spaces at this level with sufficient trade to thrive. At street level the retail that surrounds the core and office foyer to each building has the formality of upmarket fashion industry worldwide, punctuated by the queues attracted to the NBC studio and *Today Show*, or the buzz of live auctions at Christie's art auction rooms, or the constant stream of visitors to Radio City or the roof deck with its views across New York and the Center's garden roofs – another of its original ploys. This upper world is contrasted with the informal rolled-up shirt sleeves of the breakfast snackers and rapid lunch-breakers at the concourse level, at the head of which lies the Plaza with the Sea Grill restaurant to the south, the Rock Center Café to the north, the US Post Office to the east and the open concourse café to the west. In the Rock Center Café or the restaurant there is a relative stillness animated by the waiters' attentiveness, but these sedentary New York table conversations are played out against the seasonal backdrop and immediacy of the Plaza. During the winter months the gyrating figures of ice-skaters, like an animated circus carousel, brush past the café's plate glass windows at a distance of an arm's length, set navel to eye-height of the café customers. Above are the crowds gazing down from the street-level parapet and from the Plaza level, like the figures of a Baroque apotheosis ceiling fresco, staring from their heavenly perch. The Plaza is the size of the Radio City stage, which itself is replicated in the theatre lobby space, and all are set by the New York grid, the width of two tenement blocks, back to back, which was famously translated into the length of the Rockettes' chorus line. The public rituals that have developed around this relatively intimate urban stage have often been initiated by informal beginnings. The most signature instance is the building workers' installation of a Christmas tree on their site in 1931, which has since developed into the forest-scale trees and elaborate decorations that have become an essential New York and national seasonal celebration. The lowering of the space had another important effect: that of acoustic as well as spatial intimacy. Up on the surrounding streets, the only conversation is a private one at very close quarters given the ambient sound levels, which are highest on the avenues but slightly quieter on the streets; these are however transformed into a communicative level within the Plaza itself. It allows for music, speech and the tannoy which was notably used in the 1980s to alert the 'gentleman in the red top' to slow down on the ice as he wove his way between the ageing Russian ballerinas out for their afternoon skate.[9]

The third aspect of John D Rockefeller's agenda was his obsession with materials and construction that has gifted the entire complex its appreciation over time, in contrast to the efforts of so many imitators whose sparkly beginnings rapidly deteriorated to a sullen decline because of the shoddiness of their construction, weathering and ambition. Although Raymond Hood is credited with the use of limestone by shaming the project manager Todd, at

Eric Parry, sketch view from the Rockefeller Center Café towards the Plaza, New York, 2014
The sketch of the sunken Plaza, made in early spring, shows four horizons: the street balcony; Prometheus (to the mid-level of La Manche); the skaters; and the café clients.

a meeting referred to in Walter H Kilham's biography of Hood,[10] I have been forcefully struck by the many references in literature on the Rockefeller Center to Rockefeller's attention to detail, and nowhere more so than the following quotation from his biography written by Raymond B Fosdick:

> He was a perfectionist, with an abhorrence of anything that was shoddy or second rate ... He liked to measure things – to see for himself how wide a garden gate had to be or the height of a new window screen. It is perhaps symbolic of his increasing passion for exactness that about this time (1907–1910) he began to carry in his hip pocket a four-foot rule, a practice which he continued all his life.[11]

The architectural grammar of the walls of these big buildings is straightforward, part of Hood's developing dexterity. As in his earlier American Radiator Building (1924) nearby, where brick is used, the language of continuous vertical piers of loadbearing material, employed as very substantial cladding to the internal steel frame, is interspersed with punched windows in vertical ranks with spandrels in stone or metal between. The bed of the limestone is expressed by the blasted surface that creates a sense of weathered patina in the striation. This is then used to create the emphasis of giant scale of the blocks through their alternating coursing, laid against and with their natural bed. In sharp raking light, the shadow modelling of the surface is very pronounced and powerful. The blocks of stone at the lower registers and throughout the lower buildings are of a heroic dimension, typically 1,650 by 1,120 by 200 millimetres (65 by 44 by 8 inches) on bed. That makes the typical length of quoin stones 1,850 millimetres (73 inches) to the joint – equivalent to the height of a large person. These terrific flat dimensions then turn into plastic form at the framing of the lower openings through the proliferation of the sculpted friezes, in glass, stainless steel, stone, gilded elements, painted polychromy, bronze and mosaic. The gibe of the *New York Evening Journal* cartoon 'Oilcan City' (illustrated in Chapter 2) was transformed through material into Sigfried Giedion's eulogy in *Space, Time and Architecture* (1941):

> In the great city of our age there will be a civic center, a public place which like the agora of Athens, the Roman Forum and the medieval Cathedral Square will be a community focus and popular concourse. According to the highly differentiated requirements of present day social life, this center will be concentrated in tall buildings freely placed in open spaces, surrounded and defined by greenery. What it will be like in spatial organization and plastic treatment may be largely foreseen in a recent great urban development – Rockefeller Center in New York City. Such an anticipation is the rare exception in our studies: it is not often our privilege to be able to discuss the new conceptions of our period in terms of actual construction.[12]

Layering of Contemporary Cities

The Rockefeller Center, conceived from the melding of commercial opportunity, the philanthropic equivalent of an emperor's bequest and the freshness of a city plan established barely a hundred years earlier, finds itself the heart of the greatest metropolis on earth. Winding this cycle on, imagining the waning of America, the Center as ruin, its inhabitation in time again is to draw us close to a city that lives with the myths and angst of its past as part of everyday existence like no other – Rome. The archaeologists, historians and social scientists continue to be enthralled by what the city can offer to modern scholarship. Joseph Rykwert in his seminal *The Idea of a Town* (1963) used Rome particularly as a reminder to architects and planners in the heyday of the British new town building boom, that there was more to town-making than empirical sociology and product design.[13] In the book he drew together two critical strands of investigation: that of the social, political and artistic history of the Italian town, together with an anthropological investigation of how society related to the fabric that it created and by which it was then subsequently conditioned.

All cities, and particularly those of the developed world, suffer the same sclerotic congestion of pipework, ducts and cables immediately below the pavement level in a battle of ever-increasing communications demands and the proliferation of the suppliers of them. At a more varied depth, constrained by the gravitational flow of liquids, the supply of water and the consequent evacuation of waste water and surface water has been a consistent determinant of the life and death of cities. The ancient city of Yazd in the centre of the Iranian plateau, a city of adobe domes and wind-catchers, built into the ground to protect itself from the searing desert sun, has an elaborate and sophisticated web of tunnels constructed to very low gradients that connect it to the waters of the mountains up to 50 kilometres (30 miles) away. The surface of these routes is dotted by telltale signs of the tunnel works: a vertical shaft every kilometre (two-thirds of a mile) surrounded by a circular disk of waste material. The *qanats*, as the tunnels are called, were dug by a tribe of labourers and deliver water to domed spaces cut into the stone bedrock deep under the covered streets of the city. These prodigious feats of ancient engineering are the antecedents of contemporary desert cities like Doha, where the new quarter of Msheireb, created in order to provide a liveable city above ground without a total reliance on air-conditioned cars to carry passengers on even the shortest journeys, has as a minimum of four subterranean storeys, one of which is solely for the pipework including air evacuation and waste disposal systems to serve the buildings and streets above ground. Political survival has always been closely linked to the wellbeing of the urban citizen, with revolutions fed by the discontent of failed infrastructure; when abundant energy fails, these subterranean caverns will dwarf the most intricate catacombs in their spatial complexity for the dead or the living.

Parisian Boulevards

When King Louis XIV removed his entire court to Versailles in 1682, he did so in order to leave the decaying fabric of Paris to his earthbound subjects:

constrained by a street pattern of widths generally between 5 and 8 metres (16 and 26 feet), it made the passage of carts and carriages difficult. Voices were raised – notably that of the architect and urbanist Charles de Wailly (1730–1798) – to create neighbourhood spaces and to cut new roads through the French capital, but very little was achieved before the Revolution of 1789, and even then the positive intentions had no great effect beyond the demolition of some of the key monuments of the *ancien régime* like the notorious Bastille fortress prison. There were plans to create better public routes, notably the link between rue Saint-Antoine and the Louvre that was later to become rue de Rivoli.

Napoleon III (1808–1873), whose rise through the political landscape of France following the insurrection of 1848 led to the establishment of the Second Empire, changed the face of Paris both formally and socially and with radical speed in the two decades that followed the establishment of his reign. Before his political ascent and following a failed coup d'état, he had lived in London between 1836 and 1840. Two opposites of London left a particular impression in his thinking about the transformation of Paris. The first was the London parks, and in particular Hyde Park with its generous space and carriage drives. The second was the surging Industrial Revolution and with it the arrival of railways and the first London stations – London Bridge in 1836, Euston in 1837 – that paralleled his time of residence. Along with the boulevards – the focus of this discussion – that he conceived with his appointee as Prefect for the Seine, Baron Georges-Eugène Haussmann (1809–1891), he planned parks. At the cardinal extremities, the first was the Bois de Boulogne to the west, followed by the Bois de Vincennes to the east, then in close sequence to the north the Parc des Buttes-Chaumont and to the south Parc Montsouris. By these and the annexation of 11 surrounding communes, Paris grew in a single giant step.

Napoleon III's close involvement with this transformational plan for Paris is underlined by Haussmann who recounted in his memoirs how, following his appointment, the Emperor showed him a coloured plan on which his ideas for Paris were indicated, with 'a plan of Paris, on which one could see drawn by [the Emperor] himself, in blue, in red, in yellow and in green, according to their degree of urgency, the different new routes he proposed to realise'.[14] These were the alignments for the cutting of streets through the existing fabric on a scale unprecedented in the history of city planning. At first they were continuing the works already conceived and begun by Napoleon Bonaparte, Charles X and Louis-Philippe on the east–west axis of rue de Rivoli, but the

Fortuné de Fournier,
Le cabinet de travail de Napoléon III aux Tuileries,
1862
Although there is some dispute as to whether the original plan coloured by Napoleon III's own hand may have survived, there is no doubt the Emperor had a special interest in the modernisation of the capital. This watercolour by Fournier, depicting Napoleon III's office in the Tuileries in 1862, shows how central the plan of Paris was to the Emperor.

north–south boulevards of Strasbourg and Sébastopol were added to create the *grande croisée de Paris* meeting at place du Châtelet.[15] In order to turn the imperial dream into a reality, Napoleon III had to establish the financial means to carry it out. This he did by establishing a banking system to create the necessary debt financing that underwrote the phenomenal spend required to build the 110 kilometres (70 miles) of new roads with their associated pavements, the 100,000 trees planted and, unseen, the corollary of the above ground: the sewer systems and the *coupe anatomique* (a multilayered cross section of a street much like the 19th-century anatomical sections of the human body – this in a time when the city itself was seen and spoken of as an organism) interconnecting the two worlds.[16]

The typical boulevard was three times the width of pre-existing Parisian streets, with the tree-lined pavements on either side 8 metres (26 feet) wide and the central carriageway 16 metres (52 feet), dimensions that had been reserved in the *ancien régime* for royalty. To line these great streets, Haussmann dictated the architectural order in both the character of the elevation and the section. The latter consisted of shops and offices at ground floor and basement, a mezzanine or entresol, the second floor with a continuous balcony, the third and fourth featuring windows with individual balconies, and the fifth floor with a continuous undecorated balcony and a mansard roof limited to 45 degrees from the vertical with garret rooms and dormer windows. The wall accumulates to a height of 22 metres (72 feet), or equivalent to two-thirds of the width of the street, and is load-bearing, faced in the pale buff colour of limestone from the local Île-de-France region. The openings are at regulated centres, creating a ratio of window to wall area of 35 per cent, with a typical dimension of 113 by 217 centimetres (44 by 85 inches). The wall is given emphasis by the stone corbelling and the pilastered framing to openings, simplifying as they get higher into the ubiquitous portrait-proportioned French window type with its associated concertina shutters, representative of the individual within the body of the whole.

In addition to the masonry and the vast quantities of standard materials needed, two specialist industries also mushroomed: wrought and cast iron for the balconies, perhaps six times the length of the new roads or close to seven hundred kilometres (four hundred miles); and, for the tight low pitches of the upper mansards, rainwater goods and dormer surrounds, zinc. The original licence to extract zinc, part of the metallurgical excitement of the new science

Boulevard Saint-Germain, Paris: westward view
Introduced as the main east–west axis on the left bank during Baron Haussmann's rebuilding of Paris in the 1850s and 1860s, boulevard Saint-Germain was completed in 1877.

of materials in the 18th and early 19th centuries, had been given by Napoleon Bonaparte in 1805. Light and non-ferrous, one of its first official uses was the Emperor's campaign bath. Its use in buildings was soon established as a sheet material for roofing at low pitches and decorative surrounds of soldered sections, to emulate heavier carved or cast elements. The technique of

Intersection of boulevard Saint-Germain and rue de l'Université, Paris: westward view
Rue de l'Université is shown on the left, with the much broader boulevard Saint-Germain on the right.

14 rue Bonaparte, Faubourg Saint-Germain, Paris: southward view
On the right is the entrance to the École des Beaux-Arts.

extraction up to the 1950s was through distillation, which did not eliminate traces of impurities, the most particular of which was cadmium. It is these impurities that give the zinc its light bluish-grey character that made up almost the entirety of the roofscape of Paris and indeed a significant element of the Impressionists' palette. It is however rapidly disappearing as modern production techniques, impurity free, create a dull dark grey surface, a monotonous equivalent of the original.

At street level, one of the most significant gifts to the city that the boulevard created was the Parisian café. Haussmann's streets would be hollow indeed without the historic urban fabric into which they were pitched, and the healed wounds are there to be seen around all the backs and intersections of the new and old. Boulevard Saint-Germain ploughed its way in an arc of more than three kilometres (about two miles) through the streets and blocks of the medieval Faubourg Saint-Germain. It connected

Les Deux Magots, 6 place Saint-Germain-des-Prés, Paris, 1873
The corner entrance from boulevard Saint-Germain.

two of the bridges across the Seine – pont de la Concorde to the west and pont de Sully to the east – and roughly at its centre it exposed the oldest church of Paris, Saint-Germain-des-Prés, with its Romanesque bell tower, once the heart of the vast abbey standing on the left bank outside the

Café de Flore, 172 boulevard Saint-Germain, Paris, 1887
Certainly one of the most discreetly relevant cafés and esplanades in the artistic production of European culture, the Flore is still today a place of encounter, exchange and conversation.

medieval city. The neighbourhood, like London's Soho, became the haunt of intellectuals. The *encyclopédistes* gathered at rue de Buci; the revolutionaries Marat, Danton and Guillotin lived here; Le Divan bookstore was at the crossing of rue Bonaparte and rue de l'Abbaye – the list is phenomenal. Great cultural institutions, particularly the École nationale supérieure

des Beaux-Arts, lie at its heart between the Seine and the crossing of Haussmann's new interventions that created place Saint-Germain-des-Prés. Two of the most celebrated cafés of Paris – Les Deux Magots and Café de Flore – sprang up in an exemplary instance of what Walter Benjamin, one of the endless list of significant clientele, termed 'auratic perception' or the aesthetic faculty by means of which a civilisation may recover an appreciation of myth[17] – a condition as true of the Eiffel Tower as it is of the boulevard and the Parisian café. But what are the characteristics that mark this celebrated paragon of communicative space?

Eric Parry, sketch of the interior of Les Deux Magots, 6 place Saint-Germain-des-Prés, Paris, 2014
Looking towards the entrance, as seen from the exterior on page 136. The double-sided red banquette defines the floorscape and lower horizon of the room. Outside the room the layers between interior and exterior include the conservatories and the awnings.

Both the Café de Flore and Les Deux Magots sit at the splayed corners of their respective buildings, which are naturally used as the entry points; this is also a direct result of Haussmann's urban rule to negotiate the intersection of boulevard and street. Les Deux Magots faces the plaza more expansively along one flank than does the Café de Flore, which is more compressed by the ancient rue Saint-Benoît. The Café de Flore uses its entresol as a conspiratorial space accessed by a tight stair. Joseph Rykwert described this scene in Saint-Germain-des-Près in the early 1950s, with the avant-garde bookshop La Hune sited between the two cafés and, in the Café de Flore, the ritual of the waiter announcing 'Monsieur Sartre au téléphone', inviting the diminutive philosopher to rise to an admiring public.[18] Brassaï in his conversations with Picasso of 1964 spoke of the 'café period' in which 'after a conspicuous appearance at Lipp or Les Deux-Magots, [they] settled around a table of friends at the Café de Flore, with Christian and Yvonne Zervos, Nusch and Paul Éluard, the Braques, and others. The ceremonials was always the same'.[19] This room set above the café's street awnings is further veiled by its surrounding verdant window boxes. Les Deux Magots is named after the two Chinese figures who sit on high, guardians of the streets they face, with their backs to the café's single cruciform pier. The café is a grand room about 12 metres (40 feet) square with a ceiling height of 5 metres (16 feet). It has two street-facing sides punctuated by the entrance at the mitred corner, each with two window openings, one of which, on the side of place Saint-Germain-des-Prés, has had its cill lowered to ground level to connect to the pavement

Eric Parry, sketch drawn on the esplanade of Les Deux Magots, 6 place Saint-Germain-des-Prés, Paris, 2014
A view showing the transition from the interior to the boulevard at dusk.

outside. The internal corner is dedicated, behind a mirrored screen, to food and drink preparation and the waiters' distribution point. In the main space, around one of the two isolated cast-iron columns, a long central double-sided banquette defines the floorscape of the room and greets the visitor through the crystal corner. Circling the banquette, a dance of small round tables creates the focus for conversation, accompanied by robust chairs. Around the perimeter, the same banquette section with a high back, to seated neck height, animates the space while being masked by the articulation of the wall. The boulevard pavement width of 8 metres (26 feet) has been colonised by flanking 3.5-metre- (11-foot-6-inch-) wide conservatories, providing spaces that are both protected from the weather and a part of the theatricality of the street. The framed glass walls fold back in all but the coldest weather and turn two rows of tightly packed tables into three, the latter under the further protection of a cantilevered awning. The outer row of tables allows passers-by to be goaded by the ease and olfactory delight. The mute stone elevation is turned into an ever-changing *mise en scène* of regulars, chance encounters and the unattached who, in layers from the exposed pavement to the conspiratorial interior, invite speculation and observance. As day turns to evening, the tables are decked with white linen, heralding a more complex ritual to that of the day and acting as reflectors of the light in the brightly lit interior. At this point the conservatories become absorbed by the city backdrop as it subsides in the gloaming. Haussmann's tree-planting scheme provides an important secondary canopy to the immediacy of the conservatory roofs and awnings. This describes a section not unlike that of Mumbai's Bhuleshwar: layered, complex and in tune with the diurnal patterns of the city with which it engages from dawn to deep night.

Piccadilly and St James's, London

There have been hints of the configuration of central London in preceding chapters. The changing skyline of the City of London, originally the Roman square mile, appeared in Chapter 2; further west, towards the edge of the Saxon town, St Martin-in-the-Fields and Trafalgar Square form part of Chapter 3; and now we reach, within the City of Westminster north of the Abbey and the Houses of Parliament, the Parish of St James's. It comprises two rectangles and a square, the latter with sides of 130 metres (430 feet) set south and a little east of centre of the first urban rectangle. In total this is a modest 400 by 320 metres (1,300 by 1,000 feet), bounded by Piccadilly to the north, Pall Mall to the south, Haymarket to the east and St James's Street to the west.

Henry Jermyn (1605–1684), exiled with the rump of the English aristocracy in Paris during the post-Civil War commonwealth, returned to secure the freehold of a substantial part of the Bailiwick of St James's, essentially meadows, on which he was to create an urban square to follow the example of the Duke of Bedford in Covent Garden. Twenty-three houses were built on three sides; the fourth side, to the south, was too narrow and remained compromised for grand domestic purposes. The houses were well insulated from the surrounding city by urban blocks and secondary streets so that to the north Jermyn Street, at half the width of Piccadilly, forms a mediating role between the urban bustle of the latter and the relative solitude of the square. Almost secreted into the depth of urban figure ground of the 18th-century plan are stable yards, market squares and the courts at the centre of larger plots. The creation of an independent Parish followed the establishment of St James's Church, Piccadilly (Sir Christopher Wren, 1684). To the north of Piccadilly, earlier grand houses (Burlington, Devonshire and others) were interspersed with residential streets – Bond, Albemarle and Dover Streets, for example. In short, the Mayfair grid was established and the signs of its future prestige as one of the world's great centres of fashion, objets d'art and

Anonymous architect, Berry Bros & Rudd, 3 St James's Street, London, 1698
The historic shopfront.

rarities were apparent from the outset, with people attracted like moths to the roll call of politicians and aristocracy residing in the square, who had in turn been drawn by the proximity of St James's Palace and Whitehall a stroll away. Bond Street and Cork Street filled with hotels and meeting places, paralleling the exclusivity of clubs, but also with tailors and jewellers – the former both military like Schweitzer and Davidson but also those catering for the rapidly growing demands of the dandy's wardrobe, most notoriously Jonathan Meyer, Beau Brummell's supplier of trousers and breeches. London's glass-fronted shops, elegantly stacked with goods lit in profusion by candles, were noted like a description of an imaginary realm by 18th-century foreign visitors. A surprising number still survive in Jermyn Street and St James's Street. In the former are Floris, perfumer since 1730, with a mid-19th-century shopfront; Paxton & Whitfield, cheesemonger, in a 17th-century house with a shopfront dating from 1835; and Harvie & Hudson, shirt- and tiemakers, with a metal arcaded and tiled shopfront. In St James's Street, John Lobb has been trading shoes since the late 19th century; Lock & Co have been selling hats since 1765; and Berry Bros & Rudd have been purveyors of wine since 1698, complete with cellars, weighing scales used for goods but also (as noted in extant ledgers) by stripped dandies to record their body weight, and a notable layering of shopfront paint that is by now almost structural.

The ambitious plans devised by John Nash (see also Chapter 3) for Regent Street were realised between 1809 and 1826 and delivered a regal passage north from Regent's Park to the royal residence at Carlton House. No sooner was the project delivered than his client, the Prince Regent, ordered the demolition of Carlton House, and in so doing opened the whole to London. It quickly became the city's retail artery and, near its southern terminal in Lower Regent Street, met at the confluence with Piccadilly's eastern end at what Nash saw as a circus of relatively modest dimensions and somewhat hidden by the misaligned segments of the whole. The architects, urbanists and commissioners of the early 20th century, faced with the first cycle of 100-year leases on Crown property falling in, were radical in their ambition for Piccadilly, a street with dimensions almost large enough to be considered the equivalent of a Parisian boulevard. Piccadilly is one-sided between Hyde Park Corner and Green Park Underground stations, and then in north–south dialogue as it extends eastwards to the Circus. The street is rich in the variety of architecture and retail icons. The Ritz Hotel, an excellent plan resolution of an awkward site, was seen as a talisman of taste when it opened in 1911. The Wolseley, now a highly regarded restaurant, was opened in the 1920s as a car showroom, one of many in the area at the time. To the north the

Joseph Emberton, Waterstones (formerly Simpsons of Piccadilly), 203–206 Piccadilly, London, 1936
View of the modernist facade. Emberton's building reflects still today the human and urban context of Piccadilly, surviving ongoing changes in social mores and now overpopulated streets.

scale of the grand houses, now metamorphosed like Burlington House into the Royal Academy of Arts and other Royal societies, can still be read by pacing through the Burlington Arcade, completed a century earlier in 1819 with more than seventy shops. On the south side Fortnum & Mason, one of London's most extravagant department stores, is flanked by booksellers like Hatchards and in proximity to both Princes Arcade of 1933 and the Piccadilly Arcade of 1910. These arcades are the shorter dimension of the blocks between Piccadilly and Jermyn Street. At the east end of Piccadilly, the tide from the rebuilding of Regent Street and the Quadrant, completed in 1927, is very much in evidence. Piccadilly Circus was reformed to a plan of 1906 by Richard Norman Shaw (1831–1912), who designed the Piccadilly Hotel with its giant order lifted above the street facade. It was remodelled again in the interwar period, by Reginald Blomfield (1856–1942), a rather forgotten but then influential architect. He designed the stage scenery for the Circus: firstly the key block between the two streets, then Swan & Edgar's department store, but also the symmetrical east and west portals to Lower Regent Street and the County Fire Office axially to the north.

Later, the urban block on the south side of Piccadilly had its flank to Lower Regent Street and return to Jermyn Street completed, accommodating banks with offices above behind the confident giant-order horizontality of Joseph Emberton's Simpsons of Piccadilly (1936) in the adjoining block. A recent addition to the scene is the One Eagle Place building (Eric Parry Architects,

2013). The facade, constructed in ceramic, is intended to approach the issue of artifice, polychromy and the introduction of a public manifestation of visual art that grows out of the body of the building rather than being additive. The use of an off-white glaze on the north-facing elevation allows the facade to reflect the giant-scale moving digital displays that have become an inherent part of the Circus. The cornice of One Eagle Place is by Richard Deacon and titled *Piccadilly*; a public artwork, it brings creative force and intrigue to the horizons set by the historic surrounding fabric. Most importantly for the vibrancy of this part of London, the girdle of the block at ground level has been renewed with retail units, larger to Piccadilly, more intimate to Jermyn Street in respect of a long tradition of this city within a city.

Alfred Gilbert, Shaftesbury Memorial Fountain, Piccadilly Circus, London, 1893, with Eric Parry Architects' One Eagle Place, Piccadilly, 2013 in the background
Historic and contemporary public art: Gilbert's iconic 19th-century monument commonly known as 'Eros', and behind it, the recent One Eagle Place building, featuring the *Piccadilly* cornice by Richard Deacon.

The answer to the question 'What makes a successful urban neighbourhood?' lies principally in its streets, that is to say their governance and most importantly their economic, social and spatial characteristics. From the few precedents presented in this chapter, certain characteristics are common, of which the two we would in conclusion draw to the reader's attention are the sectional layering of the facade, between interior and exterior, and the kinetic and sensory experience moving parallel with the street. While gaps and pauses are vital, as with the structure of language, the dumb silence of over-monumental buildings or over-regimented order suffocates the richness we would recognise as evidence of a collective living creativity – the choreography of the street.

For our final chapter we move from the hard underfoot of the street to the soft underfoot of the park – urban spaces, for reflection and make-believe, and how such contexts can help us reimagine ourselves.

References

1. *Bombay Gazetteer*, 1907, p 354, quoted in Eric Parry, 'Ritual of the City', *Architectural Review*, August 1987, p 33.
2. SM Edwardes, *Census of India: Bombay (Town & Island)*, vol X, part IV, Times of India Press (Bombay), 1901.
3. Gillian Tindall, *City of Gold: The Biography of Bombay* [1982], Faber and Faber (London), 2010, p 17.
4. Suketu Mehta, *Maximum City: Bombay Lost and Found*, Review (London), 2005.
5. Urban survey carried out by the graduate students of the Cambridge University Department of Architecture, led by Eric Parry, under the auspices of the Indian heritage preservation organisation INTACH.
6. Raymond Hood, 'The Design of Rockefeller City', *The Architectural Forum*, vol 56, no 1, 1932; and L Andrew Reinhard, 'Organization for Cooperation', *The Architectural Forum*, vol 56, no 2, 1932.
7. Alan Balfour, *Rockefeller Center: Architecture as Theater*, McGraw-Hill (New York), 1978, p 138.
8. Quoted in *ibid* p 146.
9. Raymond B Fosdick, *John D Rockefeller: A Portrait*, Harper & Row (New York), 1956, pp 431–2, as quoted in Balfour 1978, p 197.
10. Walter H Kilham, *Raymond Hood, Architect: Form Through Function in the American Skyscraper*, Architectural Book Publishing Co (New York), 1973 p 120.
11. *Ibid.*
12. Sigfried Giedion, *Space, Time and Architecture*, Harvard University Press (Cambridge, MA), 1941, as quoted in Balfour 1978, p 220. This passage changed substantially both in phrasing and content in subsequent editions: compare with Sigfried Giedion, *Space, Time and Architecture*, Harvard University Press (Cambridge, MA), 1978, p 845.
13. Joseph Rykwert, *The Idea of a Town: The Anthropology of Urban Form in Rome, Italy, and The Ancient World* [1963], Faber and Faber (London), 1976.
14. 'Au surplus, l'Empereur était pressé de me montrer une carte de Paris, sur laquelle on voyait tracées par Lui-Même, en bleu, en rouge, en jaune et en vert, suivant leur degré d'urgence, les différentes voies nouvelles qu'il se proposait de faire exécuter.' In: Georges-Eugène Haussmann, 'Chez l'Empereur', in *Mémoires du Baron Haussmann: Préfecture de la Seine*, vol II, Havard (Paris), 1890, p 53 (author's translation).
15. *Grande croisée de Paris* (literally Great Crossing of Paris) was a term of Haussmann's, quoted for instance in David P Jordan, *Transforming Paris: The Life and Labors of Baron Haussman*, The Free Press (New York), 1995, pp 187–8.
16. Diana Periton, 'The "Coupe Anatomique": sections through the nineteenth-century Parisian apartment block', *The Journal of Architecture*, vol 9, no 3, Autumn 2004, pp 289–304.
17. See Rolf Tiedemann and Hermann Schweppenhäuser (eds) *Walter Benjamin: Gesammelte Schriften*, vol VII.1, Suhrkamp (Frankfurt), 1991, pp 356 and 368, note 10.
18. Joseph Rykwert, 'Remembering Places', in his *Autobiography* (forthcoming).
19. Brassaï, *Conversations with Picasso* [*Conversations avec Picasso*, 1964], translated by Jane Marie Todd, University of Chicago Press (Chicago), 1999, pp 50–51.

5 Artifice

As the 2013–14 protests in Turkey over Istanbul's Taksim Gezi Park have shown, the threat to a public park is an assault on the idea of community, the right to hang out or to find pleasure in recreation. The urban park is the most overt receptacle of an essential component of life: playing. Play, as Johan Huizinga set out in his seminal book *Homo Ludens* (1938), informs and underpins the fabric of society, whether through law, science, the arts or war: 'Behind every abstract expression there lie the boldest of metaphors, and every metaphor is a play upon words. Thus in giving expression to life man creates a second, poetic world alongside the world of nature.'[1] The poetic world has its roots in the mimesis of the natural world. Huizinga ascribed several characteristics to play: firstly that it is free, in fact freedom; secondly that it constitutes a stepping out of real life into a temporary sphere of its own; thirdly that it is distinct from 'ordinary' life both in locality and devotion; and fourthly that it has rules that define its 'fair play'. He quoted an elegant dictum of Paul Valéry: 'No scepticism is possible where the rules of a game are concerned, for the principle underlying them is an unshakeable truth.'[2] Writing around four centuries before Christ, Plato situated the activities of poetry, philosophy and love in respectively the garden of the Muses in *Ion*, the nymph in the haunted plane tree in *Phaedrus*, and Love's garden of Plenty and Poverty in the *Symposium*. Gardens are commonly, though not exclusively, the setting for the field of play and pleasure. In *Truth and Method* (1960), Hans-Georg Gadamer analysed the concept of play and its relation to a world determined by the seriousness of purposes, extending Huizinga's ideas of play-forms in art beyond aesthetic consciousness to *Erfahrung* – the experience gained from art, not as an event but as an integral level of understanding constantly in the process of becoming part of the subject.[3]

Furthermore, Gadamer pursued the question of the original, the *Ur-Bild* (*ur*-picture, 'original picture') and asked in what way the picture's relation to its world follows.[4] That is to say that closely related to play and the experience of play in art is the idea of artifice, of making. As a student I remember a seminar at which a recording of a lecture by the pioneering modernist architect Berthold Lubetkin, posted as one of his last, was replayed. Rather than a grand autobiographical statement, he chose to eulogise about the sophistication of the design and crafting of Persian carpets. It rang a deep chord of recognition, as I had lived with one that was more than half a century old when it was given to my father by a grateful patient in his role as Chief Medical Officer of an embryonic Kuwaiti health service that he was responsible for developing between the years 1948 and 1962. Growing up in a mud-walled city at the edge of the nomadic life, the Bedouin tribes were always present; the black goat-hair tents, close to the city walls during winter, dispersed into the desert where they were pitched during searing summer months. An oriental carpet more often than not frames an abstracted image of a garden paradise – ordering a floor of a room or indeed a desert wilderness. Persian poetry likens the turning of a carpet to reveal its reverse to the human soul within its physical frame, exposing the quality of its fabrication. It reveals an interior in the way that Hieronymus Bosch's triptych *The Garden of Earthly Delights* (c 1500; Museo Nacional del Prado, Madrid) does on its opening. In this chapter, we explore the relationship between artifice and the urban garden through the fragile traces of the English 18th-century pleasure garden, then German post-war international garden exhibitions and particularly Planten un Blomen in Hamburg. The chapter ends with an analysis of the post-industrial landscape of Duisburg-Nord, a seminal late 20th-century landscape design.

The Garden of Earthly Delights

'Above all, do not forget what I have told you: simplicity in form, serenity in the whole, notability without arrogance, majesty without ostentation,' wrote King Philip II of Spain to his architect, Juan de Herrera (1530–1597).[5] Like the biblical Noah's divine impulse to build an ark as a vessel of cultural salvation against an impending watery Armageddon, so Philip II chose a savagely natural landscape in which to build his gigantic quadrangular grey granite palace, El Escorial. Inspired by descriptions of Solomon's Temple in Ezekiel[6] – and thus paying homage to divine origins and the continuity of a Solomonic dynasty – Philip built his complex in 21 years, completing it in 1584. It has a plan form of an outstretched body: a dynastic Pantheon at its head, a Basilica as its torso, and outstretched arms enveloping a convent and palace but also containing a magnificent library.

Philip – notably described by one 17th-century writer as 'Tetrach of the world, upon whose subjects the sun never sets'[7] – was also intent on creating a collection of the greatest pictures by artists from his dominions. The inventory is staggering, forming as it does the backbone of the Prado museum's holdings today. Among the whole lies a formidable group of works by Flemish artists: Robert Campin (1375–1444), Jan van Eyck (c 1395–1441), Rogier van der Weyden (c 1399–1464) and Hieronymus Bosch (c 1450–1516). In 1574, eleven years after the foundation stone had been laid, a lengthy

Hieronymus Bosch, *The Garden of Earthly Delights*, c 1500
The Garden of Earthly Delights at the centre of the open triptych, with to the left paradise and to the right hell. On the eve of our biblical destiny, revellers circumambulate the garden's central pool.

inventory of pictures was delivered to the palace, among which were eight by Bosch, including three of the great triptychs (of a known total of eight) and one altarpiece with side wings. This collection contained key pictures from the painter's early period, notably *The Cure of Folly* and *The Seven Deadly Sins*; his middle period, notably *The Haywain* and *The Temptation of St Anthony*; and the later period, notably *The Epiphany* (*Adoration of the Magi*), *The Crowning with Thorns* and *The Garden of Earthly Delights* – regarded by some experts as one of his last works. Not only does Philip's collection span Bosch's entire career but it contains many of his most significant and artistically accomplished pictures.

El Escorial is fashioned as the navel of empire and a bastion of Catholic religious orthodoxy in a threatening world order of Protestantism within the Christian fold to the north and Ottoman expansionism to the east. Within its girth of 224 by 153 metres (735 by 502 feet), the courtyards and cloisters created an enclosed intensity and reflective calm – ultimately focused on the altar of the Basilica, as summarised by the bedridden King during his waning years.

To meditate on the grisaille painting on the closed panels of Hieronymus Bosch's triptych *The Garden of Earthly Delights* is to be transported from the everyday to the anticipation of entering another realm. Bosch's crystal sphere encapsulates a landscape newly formed from a watery womb that still protectively encircles its edges. It is an image of the third day of the Creation.

The painter's technique of grisaille and *sfumato* creates a scene devoid of colour as if seen by moonlight, in anticipation of the full light of day. The distant and middle ground of this recognisably northern lowland landscape are peppered with young shrubs and saplings, while the foreground is inhabited by gigantic-scale exotic fruit, pendant bulbs, emergent tusk-shaped tendrils and inflated pods with half-hidden proboscis, together with the gathering of storm clouds pressing the upper surface of the sphere, giving a hint of menace. All is observed by the creator in a distant sphere hovering in the top left panel. The inscription reads: 'Ipse dixit et facta sunt/ipse mandauit et creata sunt' ('so He said and they were made / so He commanded and they were created'), a quotation from Psalm 148 (verse 5).

Hieronymus Bosch, *The Creation of the World*, closed doors of the triptych *The Garden of Earthly Delights*, c 1500
Closed, Bosch's triptych depicts a crystal sphere, a vision of the third day of creation – one of the archetypal images of artifice.

When the room-scaled 2.2-by-1-metre (7-by-3-foot) leaves are opened, they reveal a vision of Eden to the left and hell on the right, and at centre an immense landscape covered in delicately self-absorbed naked figures. On the lower foreground an unbroken chain of men and women in a chaste love game feed on fruits, the symbols of sex and lust. In the middle ground there is a frenzied circulation of fantastical and real animals being ridden in the rhythms of sexual motion around the circular pool of youthful women. In the distance, out of Bosch's pool of lust rises the fountain of adultery. The order and theatre of Bosch's imagination were paralleled by the containment and organisation of 18th-century pleasure gardens – for instance in the ride that surrounded Bath's Sydney Gardens.

The English Pleasure Garden

These gardens were socially and artistically of real significance in terms of the creative interaction of the eager participants and the impresarios of spectacle who conjured from sacred and secular sources a synthesis of music, dance, illumination, dining, conviviality and fashion. Arguably the optimism of these urban concentrations of publicly manifest artifice, which were a utopian reflection of the everyday reality of urban social order, helped to fuel an

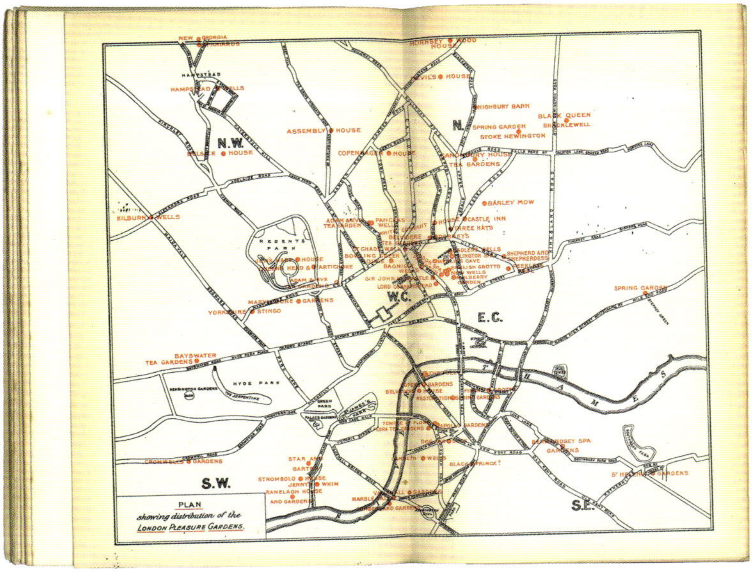

Anonymous, plan showing the distribution of the 64 London pleasure gardens, published 1896
The plan, showing all of London's known pleasure gardens, appeared in Warwick Wroth's *The London Pleasure Gardens of the Eighteenth Century* (Macmillan (London), 1896).

optimism that spawned the new developments of the 18th century outside the constraints of the medieval core of so many British cities, which could boast participatory garden settings: London, Bristol, Liverpool, Norwich, Birmingham, Newcastle upon Tyne, Edinburgh and Dublin. These gardens have a specific timeframe spanning the two centuries, and although some – such as the Old Spring Gardens at Charing Cross in London – predated the English Civil War of 1642–51 and the subsequent repression of public expression, most emerged in response to the easing of restrictions following the Restoration of the monarchy in 1660. Their fragile footprints, nevertheless full of life and gossip at the time, have been universally obliterated (with the exception of Sydney Gardens in Bath) by subsequent development as they were set in close proximity to their urban catchments. As phenomena, they were eventually taken over by the coastal reach of railways, by municipal improvements to streets and public spaces and then by the motorcar and roads.

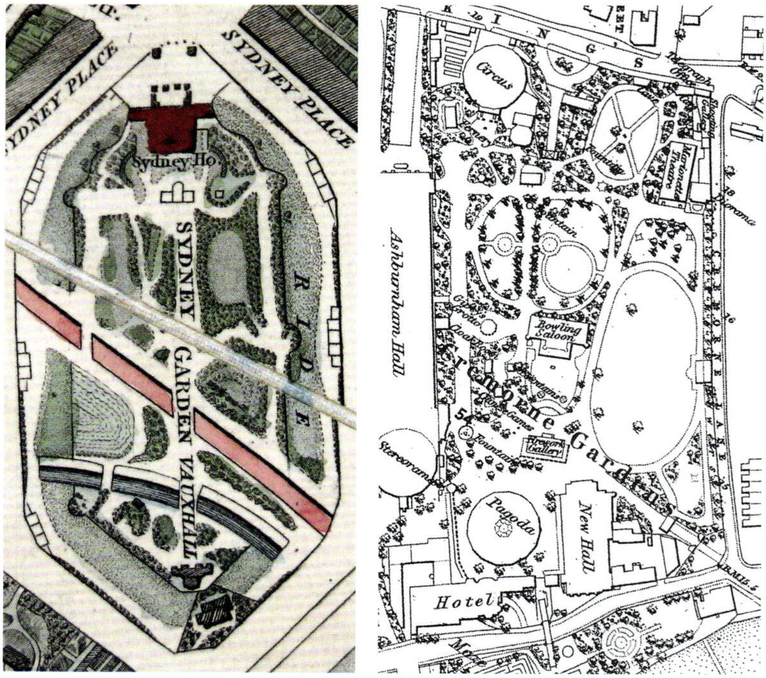

Comparative plans of four 18th-century pleasure gardens
Printed approximately to the same scale, the plans are, from left to right: Sydney Gardens, Bath, opened in 1795, drawn by George Philip Manners, from his *New and Correct Plan of the City of Bath*, published in 1841, showing the Great Western Railway bisecting the gardens; Cremorne Gardens,

On the whole there is a scarcity of printed visual evidence for most of the provincial gardens. However, a plan published in Warwick Wroth's 1896 book *The London Pleasure Gardens of the Eighteenth Century* shows that no fewer than 64 such gardens existed in the city; they ranged in size from the public-house garden described in Gillian Tindall's history of Kentish Town *The Fields Beneath* (1977)[8] to the fabled Vauxhall and Ranelagh gardens. There were clusters like those around Clerkenwell and edgier examples like Marylebone. Each sought in a competitive spirit to raise the stakes in their offer which generally consisted to varying degrees of music

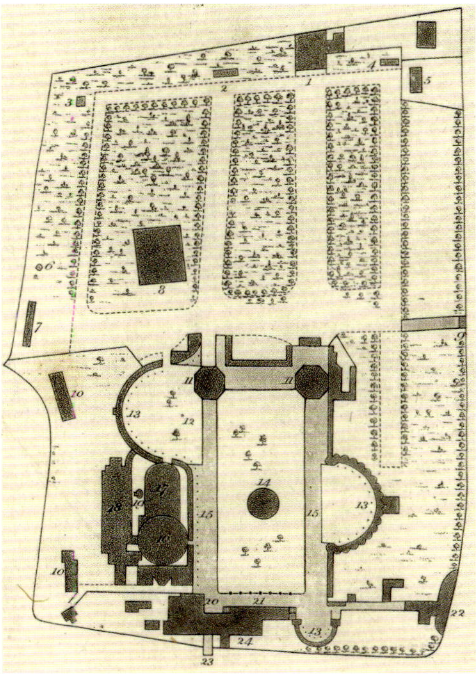

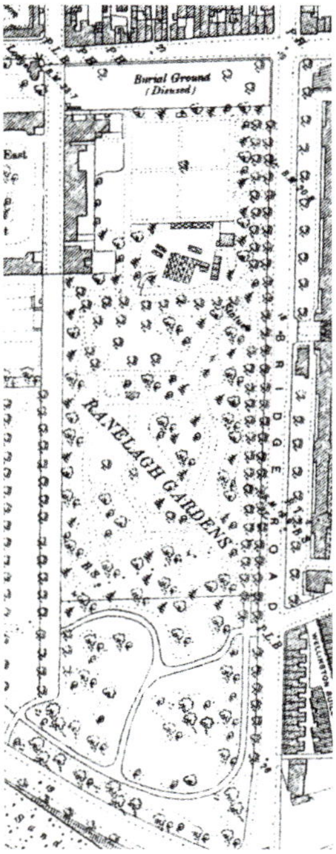

London, opened 1845, situated on the north bank of the Thames, from the Ordnance Survey map, 1865; Vauxhall Gardens, London, first opened c 1661, situated near the south bank of the Thames, from Thomas Allen, *The History and Antiquities of the Parish of Lambeth*, published 1827; Ranelagh Gardens, London, opened in 1742, from the Ordnance Survey map of 1869.

making, parading and dancing, the spectacle of illumination and fireworks, fabriques, theatrical interludes, the disorientation of twilight and labyrinths, drinking, eating and being observed as well as being the observer. The plans of Vauxhall and Ranelagh are clear in their organisation, where the setting of Vauxhall at 7 hectares (17 acres) reflects dimensions of about 300 by 225 metres (980 by 740 feet) planned with a complex structure as an ideal or utopian vision of what a town might be, with a shared central territory that graduates through a tamed nature towards wilderness at its perimeter. This was also the structure adopted in Italian Renaissance gardens such as the capricious example by Giacomo Barozzi da Vignola at the Villa Lante in Bagnaia, begun in the 1560s. If by day the grand promenades of Vauxhall appear as a sedate garden echoing those of royal palaces, the French style and fashionable gardens like Lord Burlington's surrounding his villa at Chiswick (laid out by the villa's architect, William Kent, in the 1720s) as painted through Canaletto's Venetian gaze, by night it was transformed by the impresario and art patron Jonathan Tyers (its lessee from 1728) into a reinterpretation of pagan rites, echoing experiences of the Grand Tour, oriental imaginings and the invocation of Venice through musical masquerades advertised as 'Ridotto al Fresco'. Under Tyers's management, numerous pavilions, including 'supper boxes', were erected and decorated with scene paintings by Francis Hayman and others from William Hogarth's St Martin's Lane Academy, and with maritime paintings by Peter Monamy; and the grand promenades were further ornamented by sculpture, including some celebrated examples like Louis-François Roubiliac's informally seated

Canaletto (Giuseppe Antonio Canal), *Vauxhall Gardens – The Grand Walk*, c 1751
Canaletto's view of the Grand Walk at Vauxhall with an exaggerated perspective and scale. The plan illustrated previously depicts the gardens 76 years later with an enclosure and pavilion. Canaletto also painted the Rotunda at Ranelagh Gardens.

figure of George Frideric Handel (1738) portrayed as Orpheus with his classical attribute of a lyre, and an eye-catching gilded statue of Aurora.

The gardens responded to the desire to escape the context of the everyday, in order to rehearse or re-enact and literally to refashion identity. The ceremony of entry offered a space between the two reflective worlds in an eventual reciprocity, allowing the mental and spatial adjustment, as with Bosch's closed panels or the opening sequence of Luis Buñuel's Surrealist film *Un Chien andalou* (1929), where an extreme close-up seems to show the actress Simone Mareuil's eye being cut open with a razor blade. The Hellenistic *asklepieion* (healing temple), most explicitly that at Pergamon dating from the 4th century BC, was an early and sophisticated example of reciprocity, which also required an inversion of roles from spectator to participant – in this case of the *asklepieion* to rehabilitation through dreams, the view of the city to the north and the development of the sacred wood which surrounded it.

The sense of sensory and social inversions was essential to the concept of the pleasure garden, from the heavily tainted life of the city beyond to the fragile make-believe of the artifice within. In the way that supper boxes and hedges alluded to a palace without walls, so make-up, gesture, fashion and an entry fee confounded the structures of social status. In short, what was manifest was a garden where nature was bent to artifice in the mirroring of the city's communicative spaces, and where the citizen took to the stage as a participant rather than a spectator.

The filth and cacophony of the typical city street was closer in character to an unwashed farmyard, an open sewer, without dedicated pavements – as for instance vividly described by Thomas Dekker in the early 17th century: 'In euery street, carts and Coaches make such a thundring as if the world ranne vpon wheels: ... hammers are beating in one place, Tubs hooping in another, Pots clinking in a third, water-tankards running at tilt in a forth.'[9] The bellicose taunting of animals, the braying and the squabbling that exudes from a painting by William Hogarth (1697–1764) or a caricature of city life by Thomas Rowlandson (1756–1827) gave way, on entering the gardens, to rails of light-hearted laughter, to the sounds and rhythms of fiddlers and an orchestra – or to those of nature, such as the nightingales noted by Samuel Pepys in his diary: 'To hear the nightingale and other birds, and here fiddles and there a harp, and here a Jew's trump, and here laughing, and there fine people walking, is mighty divertising.'[10]

Sydney Gardens, Bath

Sydney Gardens in Bath, principally as a result of having been drawn tightly into the urban fabric, is the only pleasure garden of the period to have survived, and even then only in topographical outline. The story of its establishment, heyday, decline and reawakening to its contemporary state is a vivid reminder of the potential that these contained urban open-air garden theatres hold.

It began with a staggering ambition that is easy now to take for granted. In 1769, William Pulteney, 1st Earl of Bath, commissioned Robert Adam (1728–1792), at the time the doyen of architectural and urban fashion with an accumulated knowledge derived from his extensive continental travels, to design a new town on his estate to the east of the ancient and neoclassical spa town. The Pulteney family had purchased the 240 hectares (600 acres) of low-lying meadow and farmland in 1727. Adam proposed a series of connecting bridges with roads converging on a circus, close to the position of Sydney Gardens, more than twice the diameter of the Circus that was finally executed to John Wood the Elder's designs by his son, John Wood the Younger, in 1768. Several of Adam's drawings for the new town survive in the collection of Sir John Soane.[11] Following the grand vision, Adam's concept

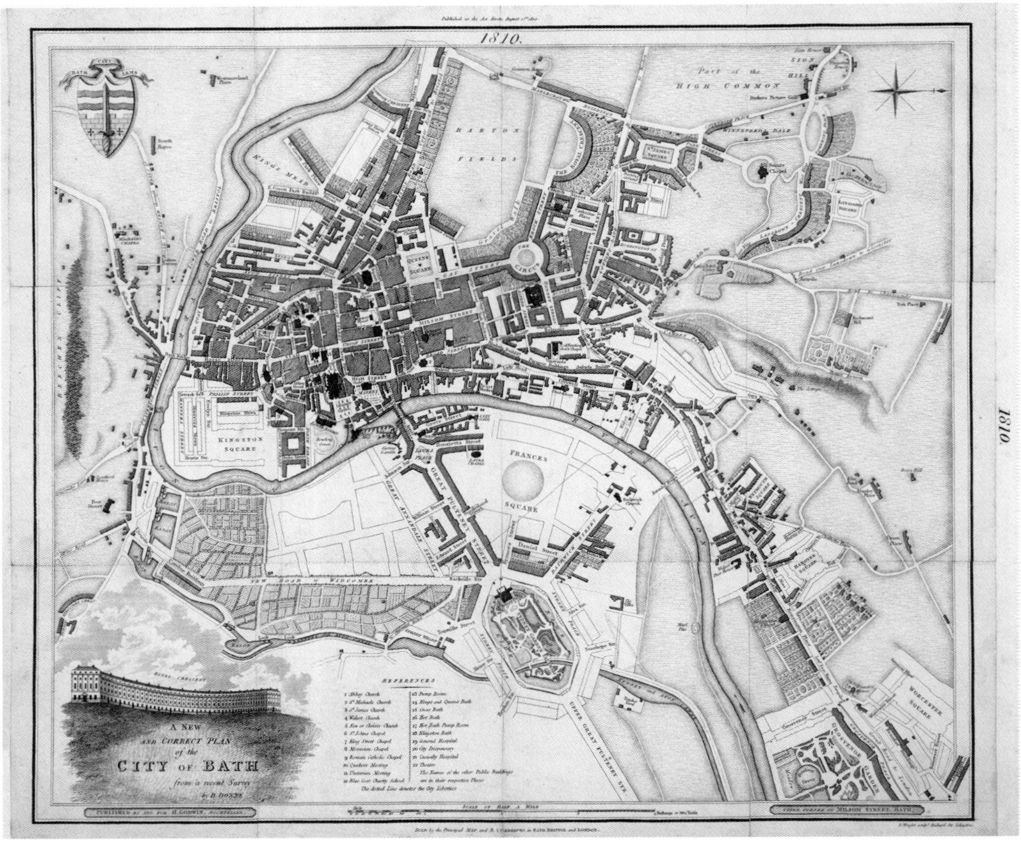

for the Pulteney Bridge was designed to connect the historic centre of Bath to the new speculative houses on Pulteney's land. Rather than experience views of the bucolic setting beyond the bridge, the idea of creating 'walls' of shops suggested a continuity of urban fabric onto the land to be developed. Although the idea followed obvious Italian examples in Florence (the Ponte Vecchio, 1345) and Venice (the Rialto Bridge by Antonio da Ponte, 1591), as well as Andrea Palladio's unbuilt project for the Rialto Bridge (1566) carrying a superstructure of shops, generally the concept of the inhabited bridge was seen at the time as a medieval anachronism, counter to the current proposals for the demolition of such bridges in London and Bristol. The importance to Pulteney of this expensive connection which psychologically extended his territory is underlined by the massive cost (construction costs were £10,739 against an estimate of £3,000 and required mortgaging against toll-fees).

Benjamin Donne, *A New and Correct Plan of the City of Bath from a recent survey by B Donne*, 1810: detail of Sydney Gardens
Clearly visible at the lower centre is the scale of Great Pulteney Street culminating in Sydney Gardens.

Robert Adam's outline plan for the new town was handed by the investors to the local architect Thomas Baldwin (*c* 1750–1820) to develop, and it seems from drawings deposited in 1794 that he was responsible for the lozenge-shaped pleasure gardens framed by terraces of houses, and with a two-storey hotel at its southwestern entrance. This building was, like similar ones in other pleasure gardens, set back to form a courtyard – an anticipatory space – and framed a focus to the long street view with a double-height portico fronted by a giant obelisk. The space defined was 198 metres (650 feet) in width and 357 metres (1,170 feet) in length, a generous territory for a developer to give over to the indulgence of pleasure and beyond the more commonplace scale of an urban garden square. The 600 metres (2,000 feet) between the bridge and the pleasure gardens was low-lying marshland and meadow, and to create the horizontal ground for the grand perspective of the street and diminishing cornice line, with the punctuation of a geometric enlargement as a measure of distance terminating in the rising land of the garden, required the construction of a causeway which was in places a full two basement levels high. Baldwin's lozenge, an extended hexagon, was no doubt developed to differentiate the space from the Woods' square, circus and crescent, but at the same time the diagonal views that result create a panoptic rather than dedicated focus, as illustrated in John Claude Nattes's 1805 view of the Sydney Hotel, suggesting a theatricality and layering typical of the diagonal perspective of Baroque stage sets. The hotel (1796; now the Holburne Museum of Art) was in fact built to a design by Charles Harcourt Masters, with a rusticated base with three equal arches supporting the double-order portico of four Corinthian columns. A central passage leads from the court to the garden without any change of level. Formal rooms on the first floor look down the great vista of Pulteney Street, while to the rear an entirely different world emerges, as illustrated in the view by John Nixon of 1801. The passage was terminated under the bandstand by a transparent veil appropriately depicting Apollo playing his lyre, an echo of Roubiliac's statue of Handel.

The comparison of Nixon's view with the plan (updated in 1810 from the 1795 original) of the gardens, which by then included the Avon Canal that had been cut through the eastern end of the garden, gives a vivid impression of the gardens in use, at least by day, and interestingly on a line of sight from the windows of the home that Jane Austen occupied between 1801 and 1805 – 4 Sydney Place. To the left of centre and in the middle distance of the illustration can be seen the swings behind the supper boxes that were reached through the complex labyrinth with its four thatched pavilions and adjacent grotto, refuges from either the weather or prying eyes. To the right can be seen the balcony terrace that could accommodate a 100-piece orchestra, its covered soffit reflecting sound down into the forum space enclosed by the building and the sinuous arms of the enveloping boxes, all leading to the complex ascending landscape. This gathering space was of course the stage where the paying public became the actors gathering for virtuoso displays of sound and fireworks, dispersing to the intrigues of the very varied landscape adventures, hemmed in by the planted boundary, and circled by the ride where the exercise of horses and the exhibition of fashionable *beaux* in taut breeches shared the intensity of pleasure-seeking of Bosch's *The Garden of Earthly Delights*, with its circumambulating masculinity nakedly astride an exotic menagerie gyrating around the nonchalance of bathing groups of seductresses apparently aloof in the security of their paradisiacal setting.

Sydney Gardens would typically hold four to five thousand in a day – not dissimilar numbers to those passing through a blockbuster exhibition at the Royal Academy of Arts today – something that the dry plans of these intensely used public spaces do not easily begin to reveal. The demise of Sydney Gardens in its role as a pleasure garden as opposed to a municipal garden is starkly illustrated by the bisection of the gardens by the cutting for the Great Western Railway, inaugurated in 1841, which obliterated the labyrinth, and

John Claude Nattes, *Sydney Gardens*, 1805
A view of the rear of the then Sydney Hotel (now the Holburne Museum of Art) in the heyday of the pleasure gardens, showing a well-mannered afternoon setting of the fashionable

John Nixon, *Sydney Gardens*, 1801
Almost contemporary with John Claude Nattes's similar view of the Sydney Hotel, this view shows the boisterous reality, with the orchestra playing on the first-floor platform, the arms of the supper boxes in the labyrinth at full stretch and a cross-section of Bath society, at the time when Jane Austen was living at 4 Sydney Place.

the concurrent disappearance of the ride into a series of self-contained spaces. By the time of the first Ordnance Survey map of 1886, the entrance hotel building had been leased to a college which closed itself off from the gardens with an encompassing wall. The college closed in the late 1880s and was unused until it was purchased by the Holburne trustees in 1912. The dismal dilapidation only reinforces the severance of the gardens from the city, once envisaged as the centre of a new town and predating John White's designs and John Nash's plans for Regent's Park in the early 19th century.

Sir William Holburne, after whom the museum is named, had served in the Royal Navy at the Battle of Trafalgar at the age of 11 and had subsequently inherited his family's wealth which allowed him in 1824–5 to travel through Europe and begin a lifetime of collecting, amassing a large and eclectic range of paintings, sculpture, ceramics, silver, geological specimens, miniatures and a fine library. While smaller than the great collections of William Beckford or Sir John Soane, it is rare in its almost complete preservation – his passport

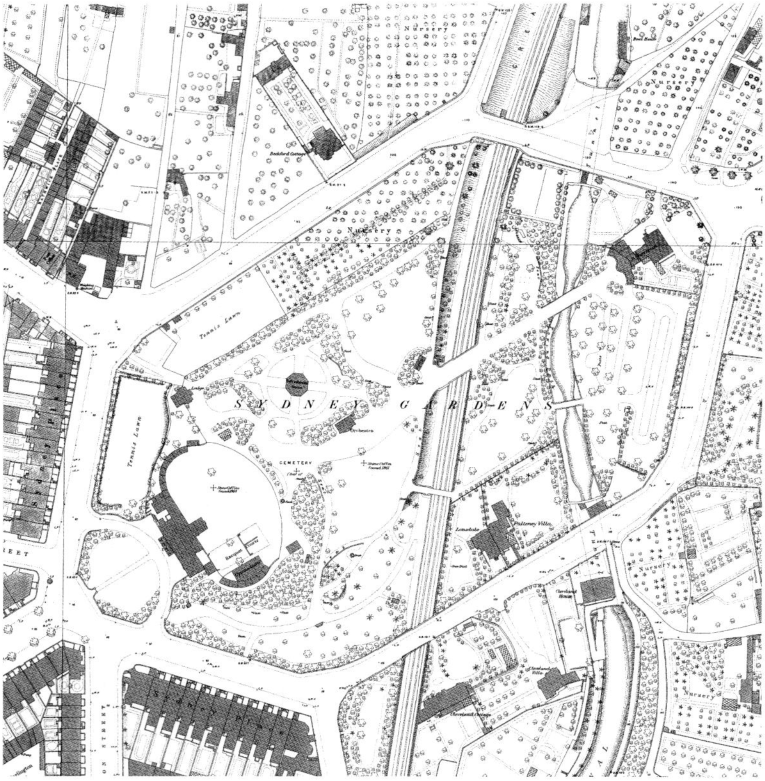

Extract from the Ordnance Survey plan of the city of Bath, 1886
The layout of Sydney Gardens in 1886, as shown on the Somerset Sheets, scale 1:500 (not shown to scale).

and exact itinerary are for instance fascinatingly preserved, as is the record of the way in which the objects were presented in his Bath town house, and the collection was not broken up by inheritance as he remained a bachelor and his three sisters spinsters. The collection was not permanently housed until 1916 in the remodelled pleasure garden hotel. The architect for the radical reordering was Reginald Blomfield, who gutted the Georgian building and created two fine superimposed double-height rooms, the upper a top-lit picture gallery, the lower a nine-windowed ballroom with magnificent views down Great Pulteney Street. There is little question as to Blomfield's French influences and sources: he had written four volumes on Renaissance architecture in France and England, covering their history in detail down to wreaths, *oeils de boeufs* and urns.[12]

For all the architectural improvements Blomfield achieved, he also made two myopic urban blunders: the first was the closure of the axis leading from the town to the garden by the placement of his stair directly on it, deflecting the entire public energy upwards into the new rooms; and the second was the reinforcement of the separation of the building by the construction of an exedral wall, without even a gateway, around the demise, thus strangling the life out of the garden. His architectural gesture to the back was a grilled and rusticated set of windows to the ground floor, no doorway, and only the view of the gardens from the Serlian window at the upper landing. He managed to rid the original double-sided proposition of its mystery and ambiguity and to replace it with a wooden formalist echo of a style of which it was the antithesis.

At the point that the museum's trustees decided to hold an architectural competition, in 2002, to renew and extend the building, more than half the collection was in store, there was no adequate temporary exhibition space (the lifeblood of museums today), the services were on the point of collapse and there was no physical framework on which an ambition for the future could be hung. The prospect of adding a new building and necessarily touching the old was, given the fierce resistance of the residents of Bath to change, a real threat, as was the attitude of the conservation officers of the local planning authority whose initial response to my firm's proposals was 'Lose your dream'! Equally unsettling, observing an outbuilding on my first visit to the site, a passing dog walker some way ahead of me in the park turned round to challenge me out of the blue with 'You are not thinking of doing anything to that I hope?' The overriding ambition at the outset was to re-engage the garden and town, most obviously by moving Blomfield's stair off-axis and in the longer term the removal of his imprisoning garden wall. The presence of a new building in the garden could be the catalyst to the broader redefinition of the garden and its life and reinforce the double-sided quality of the whole assembly of points. The power of this proposition in section became immediately clear with the idea that the stair landings would allow elevated views both down Great Pulteney Street but also through the spaces of the new building to Sydney Gardens, acting as a kind of focal lens, a point of passage between the two complementary but opposite worlds as the causeway of the street gives way to the inclined plane of the garden.

From the point of view of the town, looking down the vista of Great Pulteney Street, the portico raised to create a balcony on its rusticated three-arched base is cast into deep shadowed relief through its orientation. The detail of the stonework – from the lightness of the flaming urns that are silhouetted against the sky, to the ashlar walling of the body, to the rustications of the base – responds elegantly, as the tradition of classical architecture does, to the load-bearing nature of masonry, and this mediates between the sky and the ground. The garden side of the building is conversely in shadow, potentially evoking that mysterious ambiguity of dusk when the garden would be already in the gloom of semi-darkness while the sky behind the building would still be glowing – these are the moments of the theatrical anticipation of an abandonment of everyday reality to revelry and pleasure. Not only the mystery of light, but also the strange juxtapositions caused by the cutting of the canal and later the Great Western Railway through the Gardens. These bring to mind the imaginings of René Magritte and his obsessive reworkings of these themes in his *The Empire of Lights* series of paintings (1953–4).

The initial sketch for the competition addresses the latent power of the garden context, with the new building hovering above the restored transparency of the landscaping at ground level. The germ of the idea was formed, but the massing was hesitant, with the temporary exhibition

Reginald Blomfield, alterations to the Sydney Gardens facade of the Holburne Museum, Bath, 1913–16
The garden elevation muted and formalised by Reginald Blomfield.

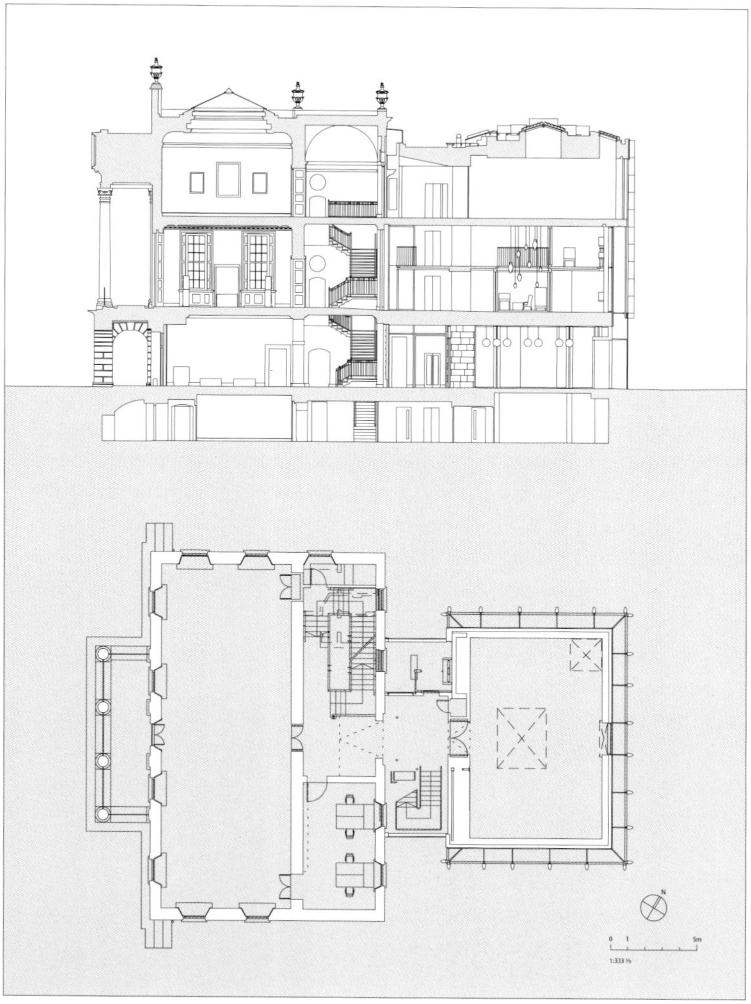

Eric Parry Architects, renewal of the Holburne Museum of Art, Bath, 2011: longitudinal section and first-floor plan (redrawn 2014)
Plan at first-floor level and central section of the completed project in 2011.

space at first-floor level and only the smaller spaces at second-floor level. Materially the proportion was a glass enclosure to a more fragile timber container, with the education and café spaces dispersed in lateral partitions. The tightening of the architectural proposal in plan and section was driven both by a clear curatorial need for the new temporary exhibition space to be at the same level as the existing top-lit picture gallery at second-floor level, and the economic necessity of running a small museum with limited resources. The essential core of the permanent exhibition – the Holburne collection, domestic in scale and diverse in its parts – was previously lost in the first-floor ballroom, set in formally arranged Victorian vitrines. In the new building it was possible to establish a three-dimensionally responsive set of spaces by creating two floors within the first-floor sectional dimensions of the existing building, with axial and diagonal views to the garden where the exhibits are not light sensitive (for instance the porcelain) and relative darkness for the miniatures and furniture. At the centre is a double-height void that is set at the lower level, very much as it would have been found in Holburne's town house as known from the detailed inventory made following his death.

Externally the manifestation of the plan and section created the inverse of the existing stone building, heavy at the base and lighter rising, requiring the largest unpunctured walls at the top and as full a transparency as possible for the garden room café at the ground. The preliminary sketch elevation was the response to the massing, showing the idea of a dialogue between glass and glazed faience in the tripartite ordering of the wall: faience to the wall of the top-lit gallery; a faience wall behind an outer glass veil covering the outside wall of the permanent collection rooms; and an environmental glass wall behind the outer glass veil at the ground level. Set within the foliate surrounding of mature trees, the intention was to develop an ambiguity of surface reflection, multiplied at the ground floor and first floor by the layering created by the 800-millimetre (31½-inch) space between the double skin. The development of recessive facades that are animated by material contrast and shadow has been an important part of the journey of my architectural practice, from Pembroke College in Cambridge (1998) to 30 Finsbury Square (2001) and 5 Aldermanbury Square (2007; see Chapter 2) in London. The theatricality of the interspersal of solid and glazed wall panels that play with an inversion of the predominance of interior and exterior, begun at Bedford School Music School

Great Pulteney Street, Bath
Completed in 1789 to Thomas Baldwin's urban design, Great Pulteney Street offers a grand vista that terminates in Charles Harcourt Masters's Sydney Hotel of 1796, formerly the entrance to the pleasure gardens and now the Holburne Museum of Art.

Eric Parry, concept sketch of Holburne Museum of Art and Sydney Gardens, Bath, 2002
Concept sketch of the twilight garden setting with the extension as a luminous presence.

(2005), are drawn together at the Holburne to create levels of ambiguity, the first of which is the virtual levitation of the building. The structure reinforces this with the body of the building being propped at three of its corners with paired cruciform piers, constructed from rolled plate sections, and held in off the corners. The stiff plate that supports the upper part is given rotational stability by one concrete shear wall at the fourth corner that also supports the lift. The walls of the first floor and mezzanine, constructed in a steel balloon frame with timber infill, create with the intermediate floor a stiff box upon which the floor of the gallery for temporary exhibitions at the top is supported, cantilevering beyond the edge by 800 millimetres (31½ inches) to support the walls of the top floor. The whole evokes traditional half-timbered construction: the building jettisons out in two steps, adding to the impression of top-heaviness like the canopy of the arboreal garden setting.

The second level of ambiguity is manifest in the articulation of the building. As the preliminary sketch shows, I did not want the surface to be revealed as a grid of ceramic tiles. The suppression of the vertical joint, given a maximum controllable dimension for cast ceramic panels of about 1 metre (3 feet) in width, was made by a rhythm of unequal widths and by the placing of vertical fins over the joints that would become like hanging tendrils, the support for the veil of outer glass below. There was in my mind an echo of the delicacy of the brick mullions that are a feature of the fenestration of Hanseatic church architecture (see Chapter 2) and indeed the articulation of

blind brick walls in the same tradition, aligned here with the metaphor of the Tree of Life, an artificial reflection of the garden setting. The height of the wall in total is 14 metres (46 feet), of which the top 10 metres (33 feet) are covered with ceramic tiles with an equal vertical dimension of 579 millimetres (22¾ inches) each. Each tile has an edge detail that overlaps and incorporates a cast groove, into which a supporting bracket is lodged. The upper level has at its corners a concave section to joint the meeting fins, while the ceramic wall to the first floor with the grid revealed behind the outer glass layer has specially cast corner sections with a glazed return edge. The irregular grid of the upper level resolves into the wind braces that support the large suspended glass units, with the continuity of the ceramic fins over the glass. At the garden level the inner skin of double glazing is held in aluminium framing with openable sections to ventilate the passively controlled restaurant

Eric Parry, renewal of the Holburne Museum of Art, Bath, 2011: facade studies
Elevation study of the double-sided (city/garden) building characters. Facing the city, stone upon stone, from the lightness of the urns to the weight of the rusticated base; facing the garden, the sheer glass base rising to the weight of the blind gallery wall of the top floor.

and café. The external veil of glass panels, relieved of the duty of air-tightness, are separated by a 40-millimetre (1½-inch) ventilated joint and are protected rather than supported by the stainless-steel bar at their base. Originally a 1.5-metre (5-foot) basin of water formed the outer curtilage, but this was omitted on grounds of cost due to the very tight budget that constrained the quality of detailing and among others this part of the dream.

The third level of ambiguity concerns the materiality of the whole. From the outset, for all the reasons of the preceding discourse, I was clear that the use of stone on the new garden building would be inappropriate, and favoured ceramic instead. Through a long gestation, many glazes were developed, all single-fired double layering, beginning with a deep olive-green layer of manganese with a cobalt-based mist that created a subtle blue-clouded overglaze. The planning committee and officers rejected this, insisting that

Eric Parry Architects, renewal of the Holburne Museum of Art and Sydney Gardens, Bath, 2011
Garden view from the east.

the ceramic should be an ersatz version and demanding a material that reflected the palette of Bath stone. Clearly, though, to reflect the tonal depth of the foliate surroundings, and to have a chameleon quality, the glaze needed to have a dark tonality, and to be compatible an underlayer of green (rather than a warmer alternative) was important. A new combination of a manganese underglaze and a stippled titanium oxide white overlayer, achieved with a reduced pressure on the spraying nozzle, was presented to the still-reluctant planning committee, and finally accepted. (This is not a criticism of the planning process because essentially ceramic is an artificial and alchemical process where trial and error, and the potential of failure at each stage, dominate; it is anything other than a generic and understandable known material.) The glass was low iron and relatively clear, which was crucial in order to avoid an inherent green hue that would have been magnified by the multiple layers.

Bruce Munro, *Field of Light*, installation, Holburne Museum of Art, Sydney Gardens, Bath, November 2011 – January 2012
Garden view from the northwest: winter dawn.

The material combination of formed ceramic with a dappled high glaze on rounded surfaces, the multiple reflection of glass on ceramic and glass on glass, coupled with the animation caused by the wind in the trees and the pulse of light and shadow, do render the whole responsive and, as intended, mysterious – particularly when the new building becomes, as the artist Bruce Munro's *Field of Light* installation did in 2011–12, a tantalising catalyst for the dormant beauty of the gardens to be rekindled.

Planten un Blomen, Hamburg

With instinctively good timing, between 1616 and 1625 at the outset of the Thirty Years' War that laid waste to much of the Germanic lands and people, the 'Free and Hanseatic city of Hamburg' constructed an impressive ring of defensive ramparts. They were designed by a Dutch military engineer, Johan van Valckenburgh (1575–1625); surprising as it may seem, ground works remain today, as they were, a large-scale, landscape-changing skill that the Netherlands naturally incubates. A plan published in 1653 shows the ramparts' 22 bastions and 11 ravelins (outworks), like a furled hedgehog well prepared to rebuff assault, which the city did relatively unscathed. The general arrangement is clear: the mouth that feeds the city is the harbour to the south at the edge of the river Elbe, still 120 kilometres (75 miles) from the North Sea but towards the end of a thousand-kilometre (six-hundred-mile) journey drawing a strategic line between west and east and gathering so much cultural and economic riches on its way. To the north of the city is the large body of water formed by damming the river Alster – the Binnenalster within the walls, and the Aussenalster without. Running northeast through the city plan are the canals that connect the watery edges. Beyond the 10-metre- (33-foot-) high ramparts lay a 70-metre (230-foot) width of moat and protective earthworks made by cutting, altogether a monumental undertaking for a city with a relatively modest population in 1600, as attested by the footprint of the contemporary city.

This defensive swathe of 500 metres (1,640 feet) is still very much in evidence, now a public garden stretching from the Dammtor (the dam gate of the old fortification on the Alster, now dominated by a railway station of the same name) to the Landungsbrücken (the landing stage on the banks of the Elbe). As with many other cities, notably for instance Vienna, once the topographical defences were rendered obsolete the significant question arose as to how the potential of these vast artificially created earthworks could be put to good use, and the choices made reflected deep-rooted political and cultural prejudices. By illustration of one mind-set, Hamburg, whose burghers had little compunction in demolishing their cathedral in the name of progress, made an area available as a botanical garden in 1821 and appointed as director Professor Dr Georg Lehmann, several of whose specimen trees still thrive. It was a decision driven by the pragmatic merchants' desire to understand better the characteristics and potential of the botanical sources of the products they traded as a livelihood. This need was supported by a successful commercial nursery garden which thrived and latterly moved to a second urban location, further weaving itself into the fabric of Hamburg. The idea of the urban garden has been integral to the city's plans, most recently with the 2013 IGA (Internationale Gartenbau-Ausstellung), an international garden show held on the Elbe island of Wilhelmsburg, and was made explicit in the city's designation as

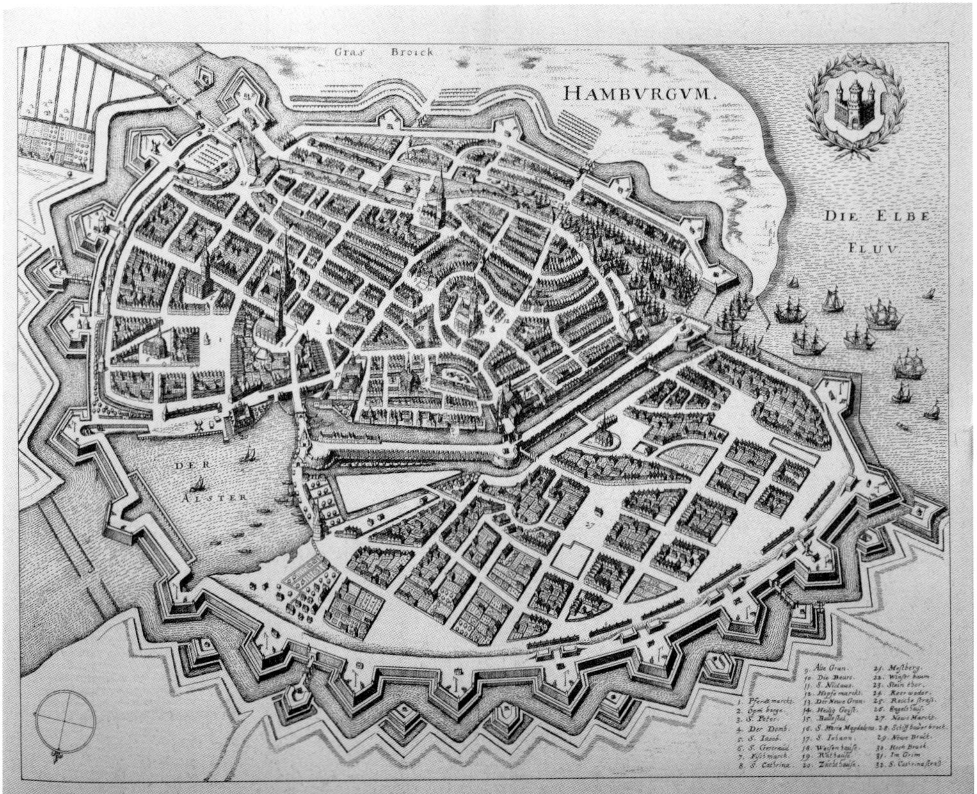

The city of Hamburg in the 17th century, as depicted in Martin Zeiler, *Topographia Superioris Saxoniæ Thüringiæ / Misniæ Lusatiæ etc* (1653)
The defensive walls and city plan of Hamburg as published in 1653. The contemporary public gardens stretch across the length of the northern (bottom) bow of defensive works.

European Green Capital 2011. The twin themes of mercantile success and environmental wellbeing are deeply ingrained in the Hamburg psyche, as the successive, layered transformation of the inner city's green ring over the course of the 19th and 20th centuries and thus far the 21st century bears clear witness. It is a moving anti-monumental and yet cumulatively massive creative endeavour that has been sustained by collective will and agreement and offers a radical model for other cities to emulate.

In the late 19th century a plan – with an urban monumental scale comparable to the projects of Gottfried Semper (1803–1879) – developed for the disposition of urban institutions along the sweep of the disused fortifications: an art gallery, the botanical garden (1821), academic facilities and a justice forum, flanked by three predictably dour late 19th- and early 20th-century buildings housing the State constitutional court, the civil justice administration and the criminal justice administration. The remand prison of 1929, pragmatically added to the flank of the earlier criminal justice building, has a south-facing cliff-like elevation of cells that tauntingly look over the gardens in which the free citizens stroll and stretch between wide watercourses, fountains and, rather bizarrely, a primary school. Friedrich Dürrenmatt (1921–1990), the Swiss playwright and master of irony, would have found the juxtapositions as vivid as any he imagined for the settings of his continuously inverting, perceptively unmasking, human dramas. The length of the next two bastions was given over to the first of the international garden festivals, held in 1869.

Having arrived at the banks of the Elbe, the panorama is startling. It is not just the physical reality of the view – across the water to the mighty dry docks of the Blohm+Voss shipbuilding firm and the robotic movements of the working container port, Germany's orifice to the world, strikingly like the topography of Liverpool and Birkenhead across the Mersey – but that conceptual particularity of port cities, the metaphorical leap of uncertainty of other possible realities beyond the immediate horizon. Here, juxtaposed with the garden blooms, is the reek of the fish market, the meeting place of revellers and mongers and the surrounding communities of the city's outsiders: the Portuguese quarter, the Scandinavian seamen's missions, the Chinese diaspora and the signs of the scattering of philanthropy for the lost souls of wandering countrymen from distant lands. The Landungsbrücken is also the start of the merchants' river-edge walk extending all the way to the leafy hillside gardens of Blankenese. This was, over previous centuries, the anxious and expectant walk for the *Pfeffersäcke*, the merchant owners' returning vessels sluggishly replete with their cargo's last haul into the warehouses of the Hafen City. A typical characteristic of ports is the bonded boundary of the customs and excise control. It is the adrenaline of this mercantile cycle that has driven the growth of these gardens and the successive waves of the Niederdeutsche Gartenschau (Low German Garden Show) of 1935 and the IGAs of 1953, 1963 and 1973, followed by a competition and implementation of a large and sophisticated Japanese garden in 1988.

The most sophisticated intervention was the one carried out by the very talented architect Bernhard Hermkes (1903–1995) who, under the team led by Karl Plomin for the 1953 IGA, designed the Philips Tower – a 30-metre- (100-foot-) high lookout platform with an illuminated structural shaft – and an elegantly economical glasshouse for tropical plants. Hermkes had studied under Theodor Fischer, co-founder of the Deutscher Werkbund, and served as an assistant to Ernst May in Frankfurt at the time of the implementation of his radical and influential schemes as the city architect. Hermkes and

Planten un Blomen, Hamburg, from 1821: plans
Planten un Blomen, a section of the larger gardens, used to cumulative effect through successive international garden festivals (IGAs) first in 1935, then in decade intervals in 1953, 1963 and 1973, with the addition of a Japanese Garden in 1988.

1935

1953

his contemporary Paul Baumgarten were part of a generation held in the shadow of the first wave of German modernism by the rise of National Socialism and the aftermath of the subsequent War. Within the economic constraints of the time, Hermkes produced a series of dazzlingly innovative projects in Hamburg: some large like his Grindelhochhäuser (1956); others modestly scaled like his Albert Schweitzer Gymnasium (1965). To students of architecture, he is perhaps best known for Hamburg's Market Halls (1962) and the Architecture Faculty for the Technical University of Berlin (1968). Common to his projects are structural innovation, clear planning and an extraordinary command of detail and material.

With the second wave of work instigated by the IGA of 1963, Hermkes won the double commission of a bridge and a permanent botanical greenhouse. On the south-facing slopes of the outer defensive ramparts, opposite the apex originally forged for the Rudolphus bastion, Hermkes and a team of consultants in garden planning at an urban scale created a fusion of the arts

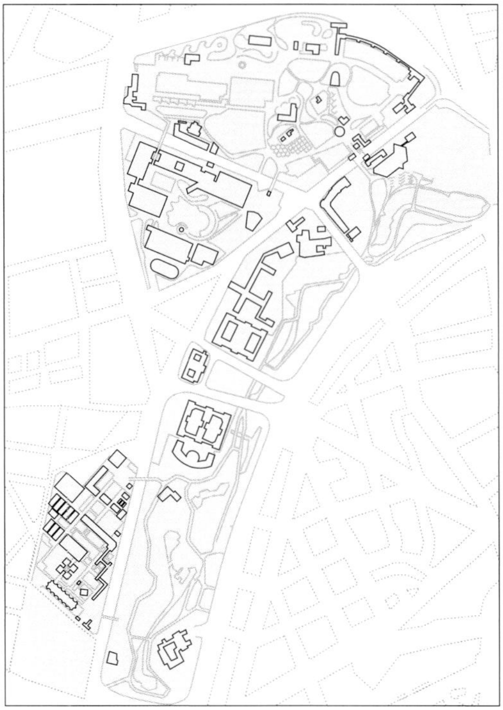

1963

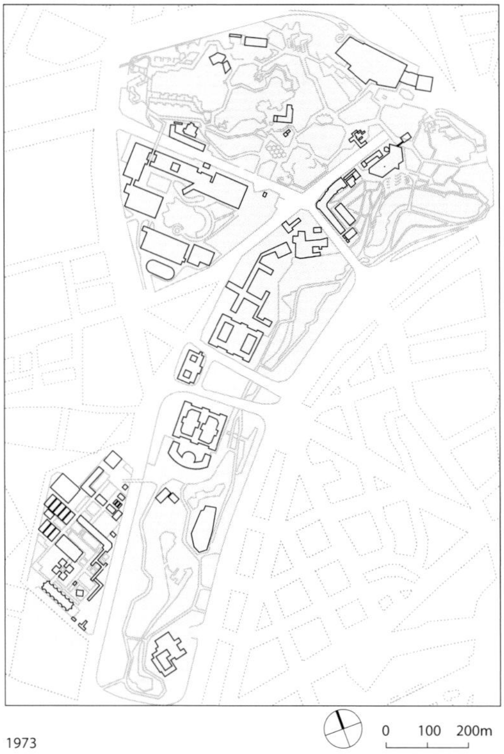

1973

of landscape architecture and engineering of the highest order. Interestingly it parallels the genius of Dimitris Pikionis in Athens and Gonçalo Ribeiro Telles in Lisbon. The principal enabling element in Hermkes's project is a bridge connecting the heart of the city to the gardens where there was once the designed separation of the fortifications. It is finely waisted in plan and section and forms a single span of 60 metres (200 feet). Precisely crafted in in-situ concrete, Germanic in its symmetry and Swiss in its execution, it hovers above the waters of the original moat below, whose dancing reflected light plays on the canted sides of its arching structure.

Four levels of terraces slip across the landscape, bridging dry gullies that descend from the new greenhouses to shelter tropical and subtropical plants and trees. The orientation, coupled with the dark slate that forms, with granite setts, the pavement and the dry-laid slate canted retaining walls, give to this sunny wind-protected enclave a unique setting in the northern European city – at only a short stroll away from the bustling city centre, fair halls and neighbouring academic institutions – which has attracted pensioners, students, workers and visitors for half a century. The external terrace surface continues under the spidery exoskeleton of Hermkes's glasshouses from which the glazing is suspended, and which with their rhomboid geometry and tripartite arrangement rise with the topography to a varied crest to reflect the heights of the species they enclose.

Eric Parry Architects, drawing of Bernhard Hermkes's 1963 glasshouses and landscaping for Planten un Blomen, Hamburg
An evocation of Bernhard Hermkes's mediterranean terraces, exoskeletal steel-framed glasshouses and finely waisted concrete bridge, created for the 1963 IGA.

At the entry level, the view through the large 4-metre-(13-foot-) high glass panels terminates at a concrete retaining wall 6 metres (20 feet) high, to create a landscape-proportioned space for the impressive cactus collection – to the right an ascent forms an arborial web that complements the descent to the carp-rich lake which is aerated by a sculpted series of water trays to the west. Here the slopes accommodate a *Narzissenhang*, a field of bulbous plants that provides a swathe of colour

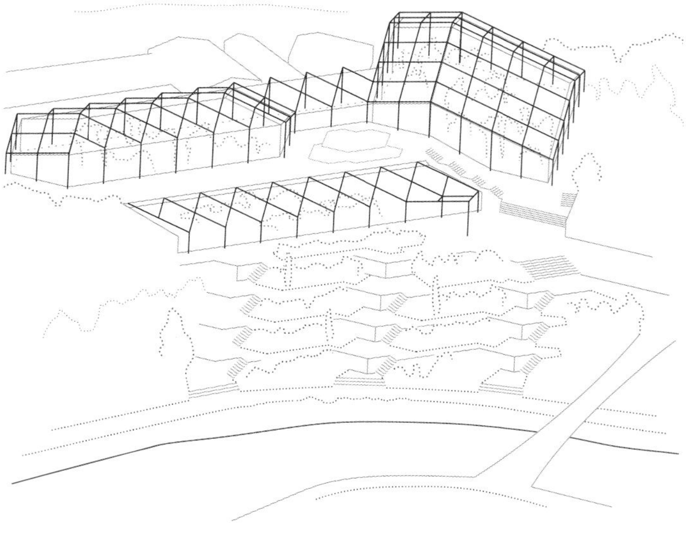

from February to June, and has remained unchanged from the beginnings of the gardens nearly two centuries ago. As part of the complex palimpsest to the east are the paths and rocky remains of a time-typical alpine garden created in 1903 by the garden's then director Eduard Zacharias. Originally the planting was divided into areas representing 16 mountain ranges in Europe and Asia – a reminder that the craze for collecting brought many alpine species to the brink of extinction.

In contrast to the gentle glass covering of the greenhouses, the 1953 IGA developed the area known as Planten un Blomen, 'plants and flowers' spelt and pronounced in the Plattdeutsch dialect of the north German coast (still evident but spoken by an older pre-war generation). The name implies the intention for the gardens to be accessible to all, and that civic attitude is continued in the magnificently generous upkeep and cycle of public displays both of plants and trees but also of the water light organ that bursts into action throughout the summer evenings, to the startlement of spectators and waterfowl alike, powered by 100 water cannons that any fire brigade would be proud of and 1,000 subaqueous lamps. On the perimeter in quiet contrast lies the hexagonally planned Apothekergarten, which includes what in this author's view is one of the best sets of children's play structures, created for the 1973 IGA and centred on Day-Glo-painted fibreglass mountains.

Landschaftspark Duisburg-Nord

A tapestry of small cities make up the Ruhr region of northern Germany, with a handful having a population of half a million citizens. Together they form a population of 5.1 million spread over an area of 4,500 square kilometres (1,700 square miles). The reason for this distribution is that the region was the focus of Germany's 19th-century industrial revolution and, hungry for energy and power, the processes associated with steel making and other industrial production created a pox of interspersed sites fixed to their subterranean quarry. It has been estimated that more than 7 billion tons of coal were extracted from its deep mines before the crisis of the 1980s created the despoiled industrial wasteland, the result of global competition and the end of the line for ever-increasing efficiencies of productivity that nonetheless could not compete with cheaper imports. The 1983 photographic record by Karlheinz Jardner of his father's last days before the closure of an old coking plant are a testament to the gritty history of labour as slave to the machine of industry that the Ruhr represents.

Duisburg-Nord, North Rhine-Westphalia, West Germany, 1930s
Aerial view of the steelworks at the peak of their productivity, viewed from the northwest. This was the pre-existing industrial site from which the Landschaftspark would be developed.

In response to the unemployment and the poor socioeconomic regional outlook, the government created a new administrative structure, the Internationale Bauausstellung (IBA) Emscher Park, with a 10-year life, lasting from 1989 to 1999, to oversee the brownfield reclamation on a regional scale rather than on a one-off city or site basis. At the outset it slowed a rapid response of land reclamation of the toxic material and the removal of infrastructure in order to return the land to its pre-industrial state, and set up a series of seminars to draw together leading figures from the spheres of the social sciences and urban planning to establish an intellectual framework and a measured way forward. The most visible of the initiatives was the creation of the Emscher Park Building Exhibition. Through invitation and competition, a wide range of creative responses were elicited – from art installations like Christo and Jeanne-Claude's oil-barrel-filled gasometer at Oberhausen; to the transformation of the Zollverein mining complex into a museum and design centre; to the new Mont-Cenis training centre and photovoltaic solar power generator at Sodingen, Herne; to the regeneration of the harbour complex in Duisburg; to the landscape park at Duisburg-Nord.

What has been achieved is a regional network of places, open spaces and landscapes interconnected by waterways, bicycle and walking routes, woven into the pre-existing road and rail infrastructure. A region typified by cordoned and poisoned industrial sites has reinvented itself as a communicative landscape of recreation, reflection and relative optimism. The Landschaftspark Duisburg-Nord has been recognised as a seminal project of late 20th-century environmental landscape design, and offers a tantalising reversal of Hieronymus Bosch's sequence of a paradise brought low to a hell by the metamorphosis of its deep-rooted context of coal-rich geology and industrial past into a heavily used literally self-healing urban park. Its success while still only in its second decade of use is in stark contrast to the quick-fix solutions of a sequence of British attempts to address similar post-industrial sites through National Garden Festivals: Liverpool in 1984, Stoke in 1986, Glasgow in 1988, Gateshead in 1990 and Ebbw Vale in 1992. Here is not the place to draw detailed comparisons – although there are real lessons to be learnt from the wasted opportunity of, for instance, Stoke, which became an appendage to a third-rate business park and suffered an immediate decline, reverting to a municipal waste tip for want of any maintenance regime, or the disconnected picturesque theme park that Ebbw Vale was.

Duisburg-Nord owes its future to the vision of its creators, principally Latz + Partner, the landscape architects. Peter and Anneliese Latz trained at the

Latz + Partner, Landschaftspark Duisburg-Nord, Germany, 2002: door to the bunker gardens
The massive bunker walls were cored and cut to give access to a series of enclosed contemporary gardens.

Latz + Partner, Landschaftspark Duisburg-Nord, Germany, 2002: bunker gardens
Viewed from above, the enclosed gardens within the once toxic storage units range from the formal box parterres to the expression of cyclical decay in land art formations.

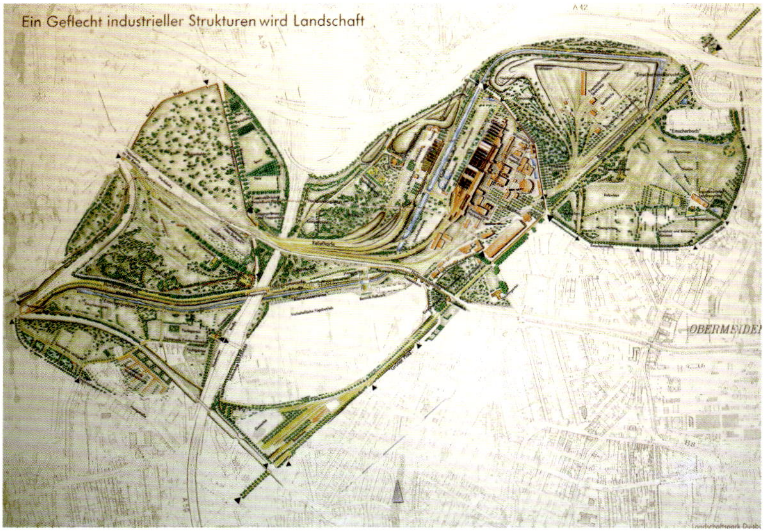

Latz + Partner, Landschaftspark Duisburg-Nord, Germany, 2002: plan
The rusting pressure vessels of the steelworks constitute a gigantic backdrop as a ruined folly to the spring blossom of the same mature trees that now form a new horizon of resurgent nature.

Munich University Faculty of Landscape Studies in the 1960s, which was and remains broad in its reach, covering the study of forestry and agricultural landscape design, brewing, landscape architecture, urban planning and the ecology of landscape. Following an academic trajectory, the Latz couple settled in Kassel where they became early pioneers of the German Green Movement. Peter Latz's appointment to a chair in Landscape Architecture and Planning at Munich-Weihenstephan in 1983 reinforced his research base in the interrelationship of water systems, horticulture and building structures. Their winning competition entry for Duisburg-Nord was

Latz + Partner, Landschaftspark Duisburg-Nord, Germany, 2002: Cowper Square
The entrance is marked by an orchard framed by the backdrop of massive steel silos.

the ideal setting to put theory into practice at a large scale and was a perfect match between opportunity and talent. Peter Latz's strategy was one of metamorphosis rather than erasure, to turn the objects and spaces of the industrial landscape into a contemporary landscape park with a complex palimpsest of uses, infrastructural corrections and mytho-poetic devices. The aerial photograph of the working plant illustrates the industrial centrifuge of the blast furnaces fed by the agriculturally scaled swathe of land to store and move the raw ingredients – coal, limestone, iron ore – that are readied through coking and sintering for their descent through the blast furnaces, stoked by gases contained in the gasometer, quenched by the water held in the numerous bulbous towers, and finally the noxious fumes from the process dispersed into the atmosphere through multiple chimney stacks. The river Emscher and its man-made arterial tributaries, canalised and straightened, collected the toxic surface water as it passed from one works to another, a sulphurous umbilical cord, and at Duisburg is close to its confluence with the river Rhine. By night the pulsing redness caught in the billowing smoke was a mirror of Bosch's inferno panel.

Latz + Partner, Landschaftspark Duisburg-Nord, Germany, 2002: playground in the bunkers
An adventure playground has been wound into the fabric of the old storage bunkers.

Latz + Partner, Landschaftspark Duisburg-Nord, Germany, 2002: view of the water park
Water, an essential element of the former industrial processes, has been used to create a new water park, contemplative as in this view, active as in the use of a former gasometer as a diving tank.

Latz + Partner, Landschaftspark Duisburg-Nord, Germany, 2002: night view of the blast furnace park, with lighting by Jonathan Park
Jonathan Park's illumination of the night park is reminiscent of descriptions of lanterned landscapes of 18th-century gardens.

Rather than turning away from the past, Latz has used the confrontation with the toxic wasteland as a physically cathartic device through a process of remediation and containment of the earth, while creating, by means of a collage of contemporary uses on the disused fabric of industry, a psychotherapeutic ground for generational interaction. With hindsight it seems obvious, but it marked out the Latz submission from all other competitors.

Their proposal involved an analytical, almost anatomical dissection of superimposed parts – nerves, muscles, organs as it were – into five interconnected layers: railway lines; waterways; byways; vegetation; and places of connection. The theme of metamorphosis, rather than erasure, was the philosophical foundation and Latz determined that there should be no denial of origins, while undertaking to completely transform the character of the place from one of untouchable wasteland to communicative public park. He strove to understand the latent meaning of the place, both physical and psychological, by a thorough immersion of detective and physical labour, and through this process came to see a beauty and potential in the industrial debris and wasteland. In this sense the landscape design started out rather as an archaeologist treats the traces of meaning in stratigraphic scrapings. Concentrated at the heart of the old works, Latz defined a new place, once the crossing of boiler-suited workers and aerial services, by placing a seven-by-seven grid of massively heavy rusting thick slabs of iron, each 4.8 metres (16 feet) square and 15 centimetres (6 inches) thick, from the blast furnaces at its centre. Although it is reminiscent at times of the spatial installations of Carl André using ready-made industrial modules, of the encounter of industrial scale and density in the breathtaking rawness of Richard Serra's weatherproof steel installations (not least his *Bramme für das Ruhrgebiet* of 1998, also in Emscher Park), or of the captured state of entropy in the object casts of Rachael Whiteread, the story behind the project is, according to Latz + Partner, quite different:

Latz + Partner, Landschaftspark Duisburg-Nord, Germany, 2002: view of the Piazza Metallica in the blast furnace park
Peter Latz placed 49 slabs of the blast furnaces' base metal squares to form Piazza Metallica as the new heart of the old works.

> Peter wanted to present another element as a symbol for nature and demonstrated it with the process of manufacturing iron, in both its molten and its hardened states.
> We used the fountain in our courtyard to simulate the process of melting and hardening with water and ice. The plates had covered the casting moulds in the pig-iron casting works. In the process there emerged structures of erosion on the surfaces looking like plants or ice flowers at a window. Through cleaning the plates from slag and ashes the patterns re-emerged again. This is the real story which has nothing to do with minimal art or industrial modules. Each plate is unique and completely different from the other.[13]

Peter Latz called this place Piazza Metallica, the place of inferno transformed into a gathering point for performance and play, literally dancing on the grave of industry.

Overlooking the square, the rusting hulks of the blast furnace structures, muscular and thick walled, rise at a distance like surreal figures in a petrified forest or monsters found in a mythic garden. Once they were the habitat of skilled workers; now they are accessible to any able-bodied citizen willing to be twisted and turned through the intestinal mass before emerging to panoramic views of the surrounding distant industrial sites and the rapidly re-emergent landscape between. In reverse, Jonathan Park's enticingly ghoulish lighting scheme of the group of structures ensures their landmark status by night and on festive occasions.

The urban garden is arguably where a culture finds its most powerful synthesis and expression in the melding of literature, music, landscape, art and theatre. As with the other chapters of this short book, the chosen precedents we hope reinforce the argument of a way of thinking about architecture, in its broadest manifestation, from the starting point of *Context*.

References

1. Johan Huizinga, *Homo Ludens* [1938], Beacon Press (Boston, MA), 1992, p. 4.
2. *Ibid* p 11.
3. See Hans-Georg Gadamer, *Truth and Method* [*Wahrheit und Methode*, 1960], translated by Joel Weinsheimer and Donald G Marshall, Continuum (London and New York), 2004, particularly pp 72, 218 and 341–55.
4. *Ibid*, particularly pp 132 and 136.
5. In a letter quoted in Damien Bayon, 'L'Escorial est-il bien "espagnol"?', *Annales, Économies, Sociétés, Civilisations*, vol 17, no 1 (1962), pp 26–7, note 2 (author's translation).
6. Particularly long sections of the Bible are dedicated to Solomon's Temple, namely in Ezekiel throughout chapters 40–48 and particularly chapter 41. Scriptural references to the Temple can also be found in numerous passages on the building itself, notably throughout 1 Kings 6–9, and 2 Chronicles 3–6.
7. Thomas Urquhart in *The Works of Sir Thomas Urquhart of Cromarty, Knight, reprinted from the original editions*, Presented to the Maitland Club by Sylvester Douglas Stirling of Glenbervie, Edinburgh, 1834, p 218.
8. Gillian Tindall, *The Fields Beneath: The History of One London Village* [1977], Phoenix Press (London), 2003, passim.
9. Thomas Dekker, *The Seven Deadly Sins of London, Drawn in Seven Several Coaches, through the Seven Several Gates of the City; Bringing the Plague with them* [1606], edited by Edward Arber, The English Scholars Library, no 7, Edward Arber (Southgate, London), 1879, p ix.
10. Quoted in Rachel Cowgill, 'Performance Alfresco: Music-making in London's pleasure gardens' in Jonathan Conlin (ed), *The Pleasure Garden, from Vauxhall to Coney Island*, University of Pennsylvania Press (Philadelphia), 2013, pp 103–104.
11. Held at the Soane Museum in London.
12. Reginald Blomfield, *A History of French Architecture: From the Reign of Charles VIII till the Death of Mazarin*, 2 vols, G Bell and Sons (London), 1911; Reginald Blomfield, *A History of Renaissance Architecture in England: 1500–1800*, 2 vols, G Bell and Sons (London), 1897.
13. Anneliese Latz, 'Landschaftspark Duisburg-Nord', personal email to the author, 22 July 2013.

Select Bibliography

Arendt, Hannah, *The Human Condition*, University of Chicago Press (Chicago), 1958

Debord, Guy, *The Society of the Spectacle* [*La Société du spectacle*, 1967], translated by Donald Nicholson-Smith, Zone Books (New York), 1995

Eliade, Mircea, *The Sacred and the Profane*, Harcourt Brace and World (New York), 1959

Frampton, Kenneth, 'Towards a Critical Regionalism: Six Points for an Architecture of Resistance', in H Foster (ed), *The Anti-Aesthetic: Essays on Postmodern Culture*, Bay Press (Townsend, WA), 1983

Giedion, Sigfried, *Space, Time and Architecture* [1941], Harvard University Press (Cambridge, MA), 1978

d'Haenens, Albert, *Europe of the North Sea and the Baltic: The World of the Hanse*, Fonds Mercator (Antwerp), 1984

Huizinga, Johan, *Homo Ludens*, Beacon Press (Boston, MA), 1992

Jacobs, Jane, *The Death and Life of Great American Cities* [1961], Modern Library (New York), 1993

Leatherbarrow, David, *Uncommon Ground: Architecture, Technology and Topography*, The MIT Press (Cambridge, MA), 2000

Lethaby, William, *Architecture, Mysticism and Myth*, Percival (London), 1891

Maleuvre, Didier, *The Horizon: A History of our Infinite Longing*, University of California Press (Berkeley), 2011

Middleton, Robin, ed., *The Idea of the City: Architectural Associations*, Architectural Association (London), 1996

Morini, Mario, *Atlante di Storia Dell'Urbanistica*, Ulrico Hoepli (Milan), 1963

Pérez-Gómez, Alberto, *Architecture and the Crisis of Modern Science*, The MIT Press (Cambridge, MA), 1983

Rykwert, Joseph, *The Idea of a Town: The Anthropology of Urban Form in Rome, Italy, and the Ancient World* [1963], Faber and Faber (London), 1976

Sennett, Richard, *The Uses of Disorder: Personal Identity and City Life* (Allen Lane / Penguin Press (London), 1971

Steel, Carolyn, *Hungry City*, Chatto & Windus (London), 2008

van Leeuwen, Thomas, *The Skyward Trend of Thought*, The MIT Press (Cambridge, MA), 1988

van Peursen, Cornelius A, 'The Horizon', in FA Elliston and P McCormick (eds), *Husserl: Expositions and Appraisals*, University of Notre Dame Press (Notre Dame, IN and London), 1977

Vesely, Dalibor, *Architecture in the Age of Divided Representation*, The MIT Press (Cambridge, MA), 2004

Index

Figures in *italic* type refer to illustrations.